IN THEIR HONOR:
Soldiers of the Confederacy
The Elmira Prison Camp

By Diane Janowski
Photographs by Allen C. Smith

New York History Review Press
Elmira, New York

In Their Honor: Soldiers of the Confederacy, The Elmira Prison Camp
by Diane Janowski and photographs by Allen C. Smith

Published by New York History Review Press, Elmira, New York
Copyright © 2009 by Diane Janowski and Allen C. Smith.
Submitted articles used by permission of authors.

Notice of Rights. All rights reserved. No part of this book may be reproduced or transmitted in any form by any means, electronic, mechanical, photocopying, recording. or otherwise, with the prior permission of the author. For information on getting permission for reprints and excerpts, contact us through our website:
www.NewYorkHistoryReview.com

For the latest on New York History Review, please visit
www.NewYorkHistoryReview.com

This book was designed and laid out in Adobe InDesign using typeface Adobe Caslon Pro.

First Edition
ISBN # 978-0-578-02798-2

Printed and bound in the United States of America.

*For Corporal Michel Fortlouis #995
of the Pointe Coupée Artillery (Louisiana),
who died too far from home.*

Table of Contents

Foreward..8
Summary of the Elmira Prison Camp.......................12
Familial Relationships..14
Stories from Descendants...17
Jacob and Marshall Taylor..18
Lowder, Johnston, Haley, Richbourg, and Ridgeway............20
Henry Ramsey Evans..23
Buttons - Thomas A. Botts......................................26
Biography Of A Rebel Prisoner: John W. Alexander.................31
Horrors Of The Damned...34
Calvin Hathcock..48
List of the Confederate Dead...................................49
D. H and J. H. Brooks..65
Michel Fortlouis..96
Tew Family..128
William and Isaac Saddler/Sadler..........................174
Marshall Taylor..185
Oath of Allegiance...190
Memorial Day Ode..211
Alternate Information - Names..............................212
Alternate Information - Dates................................215
Bibliography...216

A panorama of the Elmira Prison Camp in December 1864 by Elmira photographers William Moulton & John Larkin. This is an early commercially sold view of the camp taken from a platform overlooking Water Street. The camp was built on thirty acres on the former Camp Rathbun or Camp Chemung.

Foreward

I live in Elmira, New York about two miles from the site of the Elmira Prison Camp. I have studied local history here for many years, and also researched Louisiana history for a photography project.

On a trip to Pointe Coupée Parish, Louisiana in March 2006, photographer Allen C. Smith and I spent an evening with Pointe Coupée historian Brian Costello and began a conversation about the Civil War. A question came up – Elmira had the infamous Elmira Prison Camp – did Costello know of any Pointe Coupée soldiers who were sent to Elmira? He believed there was one named Fortlouis. Interest piqued in us – who was this soldier and what circumstances brought him from New Roads to Elmira. I researched Corporal Michel Fortlouis and he became the reason for this book. Every prisoner in Elmira was just like him - a long, long way from home.

This is a different kind of book about the Elmira Prison Camp. Writers and scholars in recent years have done a fine job researching and publishing information about the prison camp's horrors. I have no doubts about their facts about the conditions inside the camp, but to me what is missing in their books are the stories of the individual prisoners. What circumstances

The towering platform (on the right) with chairs and binoculars was built by the Means brothers who charged visitors 10-cents to look at the prisoners. Neighbors along the camp sold lemonade, cake, peanuts, crackers, and beer to spectators. This image is a blending of four separate photographs from the Library of Congress.

brought them here? What happened to the ones who died? What happened to the ones that lived? How do their descendants remember them today? What familial stories have been passed down to this generation? How does what happened then affect what happens now? I decided to ask the families of the prisoners.

I also had a question that was bothering me that I don't recall being mentioned in other recent books - many prisoners from the same towns and regiments shared the same last names. I counted sixty-eight instances. There may be many more relatives with different last names. Were they, in fact, brothers, cousins, and fathers and sons? The answer was yes, many were. Descendants helped me with some of the mysteries. I can only imagine how bad it was to lose one relative this way, much less two, three, or four in a family. With 21st century technology I found some families that were willing to talk about this difficult subject.

I started by Googling "civil war + Elmira" and similar terms. From there I found websites with people claiming to be relatives of prisoners. Then I started sending hundreds of emails with these words:

Dear (descendant),

I am writing a book about the Elmira Prison Camp (In Their Honor:

Soldiers of the Confederacy, The Elmira Prison Camp) and came across your relationship to (-----). I am wondering if you have any "family folklore" about (------) that you would share with me.

Diane Janowski

And, I received many responses along with many mailer-daemons. The answers to my questions were hard-hitting and what surprised me were the parts of the stories that they neglected to mention to me or did not know about. In many cases, soldiers had become disillusioned by the War and were absent without leave with the intention of going home. In some cases soldiers were captured by their own side and sent back to their companies to continue fighting. They were eventually captured and sent to Elmira. Other times they were captured by Union forces and sent directly to Elmira.

This book is about how the men and boys ended up in Elmira, and also how their descendants pass down their legacies today. Where other books about the Elmira camp are very clinical, this one is very personal. Families' words and feelings show just how strong Civil War sentiments still are today.

I am a life-long resident of Elmira and, as a historian, I live with the legacy that the name "Elmira" holds. The site of the prison camp and the cemetery are sacred grounds today. I can feel it when I stand there. Tears well in my eyes. I visit the boys every month or so. For me and Allen Smith, Michel Fortlouis is our adopted soldier. We take special care of him.

I carefully transcribed the list of Confederate soldiers using information from the United States Department of Veteran's Affairs Database, and compared it with other printed and online versions. I found these each to have mysteries and missing areas of information and I have tried make a more concise version by filling in as much as possible. I have also taken into consideration corrected information from family members. New family information and old information that I question is asterisked and is compiled at the end of the list. If you do not find the name you are looking for, please check the alternative information at the end. Many names were misspelled such as McKeown for McGowan, and Barman for Bowman.

I am sure, however, that there are still misspellings, wrong dates, and misinterpreted military information. I have found sources reporting the death toll anywhere from 2,950 to 2,998. I use the 2,963 figure throughout this book as it is the last grave marker number at Woodlawn National Cemetery.

- Diane Janowski

This is a postcard view of the camp looking southwest toward the Chemung River. Postcards like this were popular and still in circulation for many years after the war. Postcard courtesy of the Eleanor Barnes Library, Elmira, New York.

SUMMARY OF THE ELMIRA PRISON CAMP

WHAT - At the beginning of the Civil War, Elmira, New York had been a military recruiting depot where soldiers attended basic training. Later in the war the United States Army chose Elmira as a draft rendezvous, and then a new prisoner of war camp. The first prisoners arrived at the camp on July 6, 1864. The last prisoners left the camp on July 11, 1865 either for home or for a local hospital.

WHO - 12,122 Confederate enlisted and non-commissioned officers prisoners-of-war were assigned to Elmira.

WHEN - July 6, 1864 to July 11, 1865

WHY - Elmira had ample barracks at the time. The North needed a place to house prisoners.

WHAT WENT WRONG - Barrack space was ample for 5,000 prisoners, but 10,000 arrived so forcing them to live in tents along the Chemung River. Keep in mind the weather in New York State from October to April. Lack of nourishing food, doctors and medicine, extreme bouts of dysentery, typhoid, pneumonia, smallpox, and flooding of the Chemung River, caused the deaths of 2,963 prisoners who are buried in Woodlawn National Cemetery on Elmira's north side. (The official death toll varies by source, but there are 2,963 grave markers in Woodlawn.)

POLITICAL VIEWS - THEN & NOW - In the time of the prison camp in Elmira, the North was right and the South was wrong and the prisoners were (mis)treated accordingly. Mistreatments of prisoners were dismissed as rumor.

> *"The horrors of a camp where prisoners of war are crowded into a confined space, poorly clad, uncomfortably housed, insufficiently fed, and scantily provided with medical attendance, hospital accommodations, and*

other provisions for the sick, form one of the most deplorable features of any war, but none of these can apply with truth to the camp at Elmira nor can they be attached for a moment to the reputation or become a portion of the history of the fair valley of the Chemung."

The History of Chemung County
Ausburn Towner, 1892

History books of the time held the denial and heralded the excellent care of the Southern prisoners of war. The truth about the camp (the lack of food, medicine, and shelter) finally began surfacing in recent years with several new books about the Elmira Prison Camp. It had taken over 130 years to admit the abuse.

Postcard view of the Elmira Prison Camp - showing the camp as seen from West Water Street looking southwest. Postcard courtesy of the Eleanor Barnes Library, Elmira, New York.

FAMILIAL RELATIONSHIPS

History books fail to mention the familial relationships between the prisoners at the Elmira Prison Camp. Brothers, cousins, fathers, and uncles were housed in the camp. This list of likely and known kin is the most obvious amongst those with the same last names and in the same regiments, but there are probably many more ties with different last names and in different regiments.

- John and Thomas Allen, 1st Battery, Alabama Artillery
- Isaac and Miles Autry, 24th Regiment, North Carolina
- Charles and H. L. Bailey, 25th Regiment, South Carolina
- John and L. C. Barrier, 8th Regiment, North Carolina
- James and Joseph Beachum, 43rd Regiment, North Carolina
- Enoch and John Boyd, 1st Battery, Alabama Artillery
- Jethro and William Brinkley, 33rd Regiment, North Carolina
- David and John Brooks, cousins, 11th Regiment, Georgia - **died same day**
- Isaac and Joseph Burk/Burke, brothers 1st Battery, Alabama Artillery
- G. H., Joshua, and Evan Burket/Burkett, 1st Battery, Alabama Artillery
- Charles and John Capps, 1st Regiment, North Carolina
- Haywood, Joel, and J. A. Carroll, 36th Regiment, North Carolina
- George and I. M. Coley, 42nd Regiment, North Carolina
- Robert and Richard Collins, brothers, 22nd South Carolina. Robert survived Elmira.
- R. W. and T. F. Cozzens, 13th Battery, North Carolina Artillery
- Alex and Malachi Creekmore, 15th Regiment, Virginia - died 4 days apart
- D. M. and David Danzler, brothers, 25th Regiment, South Carolina
- Alexander and Amos Davis, brothers, 36th Regiment, North Carolina
- John Albert and R. M. Evans, 25th Regiment, North Carolina
- Dennis and Ephraim Evers, 40th Regiment, North Carolina - died 13 days apart.

- Daniel and Reason Faircloth, cousins, 8th Regiment, North Carolina
- T. D. and William Faulk, 18th Regiment, North Carolina
- Harvey and William Fleenor, cousins, 48th Regiment, Virginia
- Allen and D. Furguson, 3rd Regiment, North Carolina
- Wyatt and Z. P. Green, 1st Battery, Alabama Artillery
- A. B. and H. J. Griffin, 25th Regiment, North Carolina
- John and William Hagler, 18th Regiment, North Carolina
- C. H. and James B. Hall, 42nd Regiment, Virginia
- Charles and James E. Hall, 1st Battery, Alabama Artillery
- John and William Hall, 50th Regiment, Virginia
- John and W. W. Hatley, 8th Regiment, North Carolina
- Benjamin and James Herring, 40th Regiment, North Carolina
- David and Jasper Hester, 40th Regiment, North Carolina
- E. A. and Jacob Hinson, 36th Regiment, North Carolina
- Daniel and W. J. Horne, 36th Regiment, North Carolina
- George and Lewis Jernigan, cousins, 20th Regiment, North Carolina
- Jesse and Jonathan Job/Jobe, 1st Regiment, North Carolina
- Benjamin and Neil Kinlaw, 40th Regiment, North Carolina
- J. M. and J. W. Matthews, 52nd Regiment, North Carolina
- Floyd and John McDonald, 16th Regiment, Virginia Cavalry
- Daniel and M. S. McLean, 18th Regiment, North Carolina
- John, Jesse, and William McWatters/McWalters, 17th Regiment, North Carolina. William survived Elmira.
- C. G. and J. N. Mercer, 36th Regiment, North Carolina
- H and J. T. Milby, 26th Regiment, Virginia
- G. W. and N. T. Myrick /Myrich, 3rd Regiment, Virginia
- J. H. and J. J. Odum, 1st Battery, Alabama Artillery
- Joseph and Daniel Owens, 22nd Regiment, North Carolina. Daniel survived Elmira.
- Samuel and Stanford Pearson, 22nd Regiment, South Carolina
- E. and John Phillips, 21st Regiment, South Carolina

- James, Joseph, and Ellerby Powe, brothers, 21st Regiment, South Carolina. Ellerby took the oath and went home.
- E. B. and J. A. Presley, 1st Battery, Alabama Artillery
- S. L. and T. J. Ray, 23rd Regiment, Tennessee
- William and Isaac Saddler/Sadler, brothers, 20th Company, South Carolina Volunteer Infantry. Isaac survived Elmira, but he died on the way home.
- John and Phillip Satterwhite, 21st Regiment, Alabama
- Henry and T. M. Scott, 21st Regiment, Alabama
- Daniel and Philip Secrist, brothers. Philip took the oath and went home.
- David, John and G. Sellers, 36th Regiment, North Carolina
- John, John M., and John W. Sellers, 36th Regiment, 2nd Artillery, North Carolina
- Nicholas, William, and Miles Sherrill, 32nd Regiment, North Carolina. Miles survived Elmira.
- Chesley and Nathan Smith, 36th Regiment, North Carolina
- Edwin and Elias Smith, 36th Regiment, North Carolina - **died same day**
- J. W. and John (Smith T.) Smith, 1st Battery, Alabama Artillery
- John W., John A., and George Leander Stinson, 1st Battery, Alabama. John A. was released.
- A., Maston, N., and Alex Strickland, 36th Regiment, North Carolina
- Alex, Jackson and James Tew, 51st Regiment, North Carolina - descendants say they were not brothers - but possibly cousins. See page 128.
- Andrew and Francis Thompson, 1st Battery, Alabama Artillery
- H. and James A. Thompson, 12th Regiment, Alabama, and Thomas P. Thompson, 13th Regiment, Virginia - descendants believe Thomas P. was the father of James A.
- J. B. and P. J. Vinson, 1st Battery, Alabama Artillery
- Hardy and James Ward, 1st Battery, Alabama Artillery
- Benjamin and L. Wilder, 25th Regiment, South Carolina
- J. L. and John J. Willets, 36th Regiment, North Carolina
- E. S., J. R., and Joshua Williamson, 36th Regiment, North Carolina

Stories from Descendants

Jacob and Marshall Taylor
Company A 37th North Carolina Infantry

Submitted by Wayne Taylor, great-great-great-grand nephew

My Taylor family moved to Ashe County, North Carolina around 1802 from the North Carolina/South Carolina border. Isaac Taylor received the land around Horse Creek for his service in the Revolution. His son William inherited this land and raised nine boys with his wife Susan. Six of those boys served in the Confederate army.

Although the American Civil War was the result of the institute of slavery, each soldier has his own reason for enlisting and fighting. In the South, some fought to keep their way of life, others fought to repel an invading army, but many young men for glory. In these young men's minds the war would be quick and fantastic. They would leave home poor farm boys and return heroes. They never could have imagined what the end of this war would bring to themselves and the South.

Marshall was the youngest son to join the army. He enlisted on March 11, 1864 at Liberty Mills, Virginia (the 37th's winter camp. Marshall had enlisted with the promise of payment of $12 a month. He never received any payment. In May, federal forces, under General Grant, crossed the Rappahannock River. From May 4 to 7, the 37th engaged in what became known as the "Battle of the Wilderness."

A few days later, the Southern forces dug in at Spotsylvania Courthouse creating a defensive works known as the "Mule Shoe." Twelve union regiments assaulted and penetrated the works, only to be turned back. On Thursday, May 12, Grant sent 20,000 troops into what veterans would call one of the darkest days of the war. "I never expect to be fully believed when I tell of the horrors of Spotsylvania," wrote one federal soldier of his ghastly experience. "The Battle of Thursday was one of the bloodiest that ever dyed God's footstool with human gore."

The attack had begun at dawn, and by midnight most of the Mule Shoe and many of her defenders had been captured. Unfortunately for Marshall, he was one of the 4,000 prisoners taken that day. Marshall was sent to Belle Plains, then on to Point Lookout, Maryland arriving there on May 17. He was transferred to Elmira Prison in New York on August 8, 1864. Elmira was known as "Hell-Mira" because of the horrific living conditions. Marshall died August 29 of pneumonia, and lies buried in the Woodlawn Cemetery.

Jacob and his brother Harrison were victims of the Conscription law and entered into service on September 25, 1862. Fortunately for Jacob, he would miss the Battle of Fredericksburg, being interred at the 3rd Division hospital. He received a furlough until February 28, 1863 to return home. Jacob decided not to return to service and was listed as a deserter on the July muster roll. At this time, it is not known whether he rejoined another regiment or stayed home the rest of the war. Jacob received his "wound" while disembarking from a troop train near Richmond, Virginia. He quoted on his pension application, "I was riding on the train and was pushed off by a Lieutenant and broke my leg. I was sent to the hospital for 4 months." Jacob lived a long life with two wives and many children. He is buried in Ashe County. See more on page 185.

A photograph of Jacob Taylor and his second wife Nancy Vanover. Image courtesy of Wayne Taylor.

Ancestors and the Elmira Prison Camp
Lowder, Johnston, Haley, Richbourg, and Ridgeway

Submitted by Cynthia Parker, Sumter, South Carolina

Listed below, you will find bits of lore that I have encountered about relatives of mine who were captured and sent to Elmira. There is even one family (not in my direct line, but a Ridgeway family) who named a girl child, Elmira, so as to never forget.

My great-great-great-grandfather, James Owens Lowder, was captured at Fort Fisher, North Carolina on January 15, 1865. He appears on a roll of Prisoners of War who arrived at Elmira on January 30, 1865. He was released July 3, 1865. The signature of J.O. Lowder appears on the Oath of Allegiance to the United States that was subcribed and sworn to at Elmira on July 3, 1865.

Residence: Kingstree, South Carolina; Complexion: Dark; Hair: Dark; Eyes: Hazel; Height: 5 feet 8 inches.

Lowder served with Company I of the 25th Regiment, CSA from May 1863 until he was captured at Fort Fisher. He was held in Elmira Prison in New York State until the end of the war. Sadly, a little over a year after leaving Elmira he died when a tornado struck

Image courtesy of the National Archives, Washington, DC. NARA M267

his farm in Clarendon County. The fierce winds felled a tree in the yard of his home. Family lores tells us that he held his little daughter in his arms and protected her with his body when was struck down. (I also read an account of this in a copy of an old local newspaper in the archives here, which verified our family "legend.") His wife, Mellerson Alice Ridgeway Lowder was pregnant with my great-great-grandfather, John Owens Lowder, at the time. He was safely born on February 9, 1867, living and going forward to carry on the Lowder name in Clarendon County.

John James Johnston born on December 27, 1823 and died at Elmira on December 16, 1864. He was a first cousin of Mellerson Lowder, the widow of my Lowder great-great-great-grandfather mentioned above. I do not know very much about him.

My great-great-great-grandfather Harvey V. Haley [spelled H.A. Hailey on list] was captured at Fort Fisher, North Carolina on January 15, 1865.

Received at Elmira, New York as Prisoner of War Mar. 12, 1865: Died of diarrehea Mar. 13, 1865: Buried at Elmira Prison in grave #1963. [#1821 on list]

H.V. Haley enlisted for Confederate service in Company I of the 25th Regiment of the South Carolina Volunteers at Camp Harlee, Georgetown, South Carolina on January 1, 1862 for three years or the duration of the war. Prior to that he had served in the Clarendon Guard.

My great-great-grandfather, Joseph Edward Richbourg, enlisted for Confederate Service with Company I, 25th Regiment South Carolina Volunteers at Camp Harlee in Georgetown, South Carolina on January 1, 1862. He enlisted for three years or the duration of the war. He was a private when captured at Fort Fisher. He was imprisoned at Elmira until the end of the war according to South Carolina State Archives Civil War Pension Application #2721. He was a farmer and a Clarendon County magistrate after the war.

Joseph Newton Ridgeway was a cousin of my great-great-grandfather, Peter Edward Ridgeway. He enlisted for confederate service on January 1, 1862 in Company I, 25th Regiment of the South Carolina Volunteers at Camp Harlee in Georgetown, South Carolina.

January 15, 1865: Captured at Ft. Fisher, North Carolina.
January 30, 1865: Received at Elmira Prison, New York .
March 14, 1865: Transferred for exchange, paroled at Elmira and sent to James River.

John Ridgeway, brother of my great-great-grandfather, Peter Edward Ridgeway, did not survive. He, too, rests at Elmira, far away from his Clarendon County home.

Sergeant Reuben F. Ridgeway, another brother of my great-great-great-grandfather, Peter Edward Ridgeway, enlisted for Confederate Service at Camp Stono. He enlisted with Company I of the 25th Regiment South Carolina Volunteers for three years or until the end of the war.

Jan. 15, 1865: captured at Ft. Fisher, North Carolina
Jan. 30, 1865: received at Elmira
Feb. 20, 1865: Transferred and sent to James River for exchange
May 15, 1865: Appears on report of parolees given as Prisoners of War by D.M. Evans, Col. 20 New York Cavalry from the 15 of May, inclusive.

My great-great-grandfather, Peter Edward Ridgeway, served with the Cavalry. He surrendered with Lee's Army at Appomatox but many of his brothers and cousins served with the 25th Regiment, Company I.

Henry Ramsey Evans

Submitted by John Enos Evans, great-grandson

My grandmother must have really loved and respected her father-in-law, Henry, because she is the source of most of my information. She told me about Shiloh, Chickamauga, Atlanta and Elmira. She didn't have exact dates and all the names of people and places in her stories. Yet, as I study history I hear her voice. I don't think she ever said "Foster's Pond" but when I read about it I find what she told me. Many years ago, when you had to do research in archives and libraries, I went to Tallahassee and got a copy of Henry's pension application file. Since then I've waded through a lot of on-line literature and some well documented histories, after action reports, etc. That filled in names, dates, and places but it didn't replace her heart-felt stories about a man she knew personally. I now have a grandson and am trying to write a family history for him with footnotes, end notes, bibliography, etc. but I also hope he remembers the stories I tell him.

Henry Ramsey Evans, a son of Enos and Kizziah Evans, was born Monday April 10, 1840 in Walton County, Florida. On January 10, 1861 Florida seceded from the Union. Henry enlisted February 28, 1861 at Eucheeanna and served as a Corporal in the Infantry of the Confederate States Army, 1st Florida Infantry Regiment, Company D under the command of Captain L. McKinnon. They marched to Alaqua and rode boats down the river and across the bay to the southern bank of Choctawhatchie Bay to set up Camp Walton on the Gulf of Mexico. Their camp was on and around an old Indian mound there that provided a clear view of the surrounding area.

The 1st Florida fought under Brigadier General Richard H. Anderson in the battle of Santa Rosa Island, Florida on October 9, 1861. The 1st Florida was made part of the Army of Pensacola on October 22, 1861 and placed under the command of Major-General Braxton Bragg.

Major T. A. McDonell led the 1st Florida into battle at Shiloh, Tennessee April 6-7, 1862 where they served as part of Brigadier General Patton Anderson's Second Brigade, Brigadier General Daniel Ruggles' First Division,

Major General Braxton Bragg's Second Corps of General Albert S. Johnston's Army of Mississippi. General Johnston was killed the first day. Major T. A. McDonell was borne wounded from the field before the action had fairly begun and the command of the 1st Florida devolved upon Captain W. G. Poole, who bore himself most gallantly throughout the two days' conflict. It was there at Shiloh that the "Rebel Yell" was first employed.

The 1st Florida later fought in the battles of Vaden, Mississippi in June of 1862, Chattanooga, Tennessee in September 1862, and Perryville, Kentucky on October 8, 1862.

On November 20, 1862 The Army of Mississippi was renamed "The Army of Tennessee" with General Braxton Bragg as its commander. The 1st Florida fought as part of this army the at Stones River, Murfreesboro, Tennessee December 31, 1862 -January 2, 1863 and Chickamauga, Georgia September 19-21, 1863 where the 1st Florida was instrumental in the successes of the second day, as they helped break several battle lines of the enemy. Chickamauga was the biggest battle ever fought in Georgia.

The 1st Florida was also engaged with The Army of Tennessee at Missionary Ridge, Tennessee November 23-27, 1863 where the Union army inflicted a significant defeat on Bragg forcing him to abandon the siege of Chattanooga and withdraw again into northern Georgia. Shortly thereafter, General Bragg was replaced as commander of the Army of Tennessee by General Joseph E. Johnston.

By the time they fought the hundred days' battles in the defense of Atlanta, Georgia May-September 1864, the 1st Florida, that had been a brigade at Shiloh, was now at less than regimental strength. This campaign included the battles of Resaca, Georgia from May 14-15, New Hope Church on May 25, Marietta, Georgia on May 26, Pine Hill, Georgia from June 11-14, Lost Mountain, Georgia from June 15-16, and Kennesaw Mountain on June 17.

On July 17, 1864 General John Bell Hood assumed command of The Army of Tennessee. The 1st Florida fought with him at Peach Tree Creek from July 19-20, the Battle of Atlanta on July 22, Utoy Creek from August 5-7, Jonesborough, Georgia on August 31, and Lovejoy Station, Georgia from September 2-5, 1864. By this time there wasn't much left of the old 1st Florida.

While on a sick furlough, Corporal Henry R. Evans was captured on

September 28, 1864 near Vernon, Florida during Brigadier General Alexander Sandor Asboth's raid from Pensacola into Mariana. He was forwarded by the steamer "Clinton" from Ship Island, Mississippi to Fort Columbus, New York and held as a prisoner of war at the Elmira Prison Camp until released on July 7, 1865 after he finally signed an oath of allegiance.

Those who endured Elmira's squalor and harsh cruelties referred to it as "Hellmira" because of the inhuman treatment they received there. It was a filthy cesspool in summer and frozen in winter. The winter of 1864-65 was one of the harshest on record and especially cold to the Florida boys. In 1865 the daily ration was reduced to bread and water. Henry suffered from scurvy and dysentery while imprisoned. A quarter of the Confederate soldiers who were imprisoned at Elmira are buried there.

An old family story says that after release Henry R. Evans had to walk home. When he finally got home, his brothers and sisters didn't recognize him. Some young ones there ran to the house and told Kizziah that a man was coming up the road. She took off her apron and walked to the front gate. From there she recognized her son, through the gate open, and ran to greet him. He was just a thin shell of a man but he was home and he was alive. Now it was time to start over.

On December 29, 1869 Henry Ramsey Evans married Elizabeth, a daughter of Jesse Evans and Elizabeth Infinger. They had seven children, all born in Walton County, Florida and reared in the Methodist faith. Those children were never allowed to wear blue clothing.

Henry R. Evans died Sunday February 6, 1927 at 9:00 in the morning. He and Elizabeth are buried in the Black Creek Cemetery near Freeport in Walton County, Florida.

Buttons
Thomas A. Botts: An American Civil War Confederate Prisoner

By Hudson Alexander, great-grandnephew of John Williamson Alexander

A thick, gray sky hung over south-central New York State this dead winter's day in early 1864. Against the darkness and the season's barren landscape, Elmira Prison looked particularly gloomy. Indeed, Confederate prisoners there were freezing, starving, and sick, clinging desperately to their lives.

On the surface, the widespread suffering seemed to have little effect on one of the prisoners. An icy wind blowing through his long, dark beard, he strolled nonchalantly about the compound alone. Snowflakes frosted the shoulders of his coat, a strange garment that said more about him than any words ever could.

Thomas A. Botts, photograph courtesy of Hudson Alexander.

"He was a large fine specimen of a man and wore a long-tailed coat of brown jeans," wrote fellow prisoner John Williamson Alexander of the 5th Virginia Cavalry. "He had a mania for buttons--sewn on every available spot of his coat--hundreds of buttons from every state in the union. You could not put down the point of your finger without touching a button."

Prisoners and guards alike wondered aloud about the unusual coat. "The Yanks plied him with questions," Alexander wrote. "He hesitated and did not want to hurt any feelings. After being hard-pressed, he told them that every time he killed a Yank, he sewed on a button--and this was his second coat!"

Identified simply as "Buttons," the mysterious eccentric turned up over the years in diary after diary and memoir after memoir. Alexander remembered him as "playful as a kitten." One writer recalled a "strange character" who "fairly glistened" in the sunshine.

A true testament to Buttons's legendary status was the number of apocryphal stories that featured him as protagonist. One of these fabricated accounts, published in *Confederate Veteran* magazine in 1926, described how he had escaped Elmira by feigning death. According to that article, Buttons lay in a coffin that was en route to the cemetery beyond the prison grounds for internment. Suddenly, he popped open the casket lid, frightening the burial party off into the adjacent woods. He then climbed out and ran away to reunite with the Confederate army.

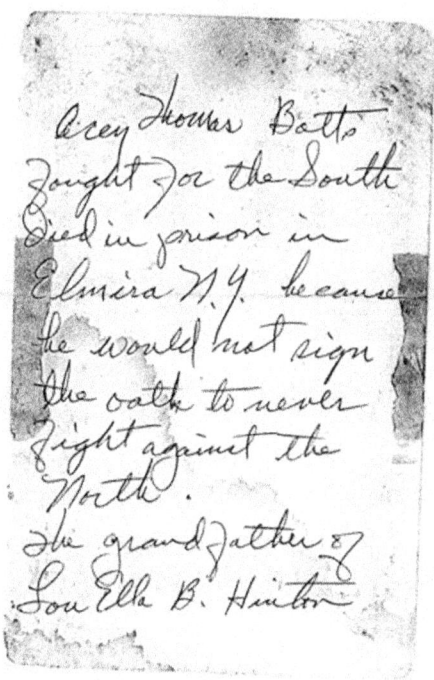

Back of photograph.

Despite all the references to "Buttons," his true identity remained a mystery. Fellow Elmira prisoners had given him the nickname almost immediately upon his arrival, and for obvious reasons, they remembered it long after they had forgotten his given name. The phenomenon was common among former prisoners trying to record their prison experiences for posterity.

The truth behind the legend of Buttons might have been lost forever if not for a woman named Annie Alexander Johnson. A member of the United Daughters of the Confederacy, she urged her brother to record his memories of his days as a Confederate soldier and prisoner of war. To please his sister, Alexander sketched out the story of his Civil War experience. Once completed, the document lay forgotten in old family files until a descendant in Matthews, North Carolina, discovered it.

In his manuscript, Alexander states that he left his father's farm in Pond Field, just outside Gaffney, South Carolina, and enlisted in the Confederate army at Orangeburg on June 4, 1861. After serving as a private in Company G of the 5th South Carolina Infantry for ten months, which included the war's opening campaign at Manassas, Virginia, he transferred to Company G of the 5th Virginia Cavalry. During the Battle of Yellow Tavern on May 11, 1864, Alexander was captured. Sent to prison at Point Lookout, Maryland, he remained there for three months before being moved north to Elmira.

It was at Point Lookout that Alexander met Buttons. Fortunately for us, Alexander remembered more than his comrade's nickname, and in the latter pages of his manuscript, he provided the key to the Buttons mystery. Describing the death and disease so prevalent at Elmira, he wrote, "among those who died now of the writer's acquaintance was: that gentle soul, Botts, familiarly called 'Buttons'..."

Further research revealed that "Botts" was Thomas A. Botts, born in 1817 at Abbeville District in South Carolina. He was one of eleven children born to Thomas Cromer Botts and Nancy Moore Botts. No other details have surfaced about his early life.

Information about his adult years is hardly more enlightening. At one point, he was listed as an "overseer" of a farm. On Christmas Eve 1848, he married Matilda Wright at Abbeville. The couple had five children: James (1849), John (1851), Nancy (1857), Asa N. (1859), and E.G., whose exact year of birth is unknown.

As the clouds of war darkened over the North and South, Botts decided to join the Confederate army. On December 28, 1861, he enlisted in South Carolina's Holcombe Legion Infantry Battalion at Camp Hamilton. The 44-year-old private was assigned to the regiment's Company F. The following March, he re-enlisted for two more years. The last time Botts saw his family and home was during a brief period between March 6 and April 31, 1862, when military records listed him as "home on leave of absence." Several Botts family descendants speculate that he may have fathered the last of his five children during this furlough.

Later in the war, when Confederate troops were entrenched in defense of Petersburg, Virginia, Botts was captured at Jarrett's Station on May 8, 1864. His first place of confinement is unknown, but many prisoners captured in Virginia about the same time were briefly held at Fortress Monroe, at the tip of the Virginia Peninsula. Soon, Botts was at Point Lookout and on August 17, 1864, was moved to Elmira. He died there on May 14, 1865, less than two weeks before President Andrew Johnson ordered prisoners released. The official cause of death was listed as "rheumatism." Alexander's memoir recalls some of the burial ritual performed for Botts and the nearly three thousand others who died at Elmira:

> ...*I went to the Dead House often, and his [a Reverend Eddy, chaplain of a Texas regiment] was the last kindly act done for our dead. After they were placed in their coffins, he regulated the wooden shavings, which served for pillows for their last long sleep. This done, those rough grizzled carpenters, who were so familiar with death, formed a line with hats off while this good man repeated short burial services--the last and only service I ever heard while there. This done, the carpenters again got busy and the lids of the coffins were speedily nailed down.*

The caskets were then buried at Woodlawn Cemetery, adjacent to the prison compound. That 2.5-acre piece of land was the final resting place for most of the 2,917 who did not survive the rigors of Elmira. In plot No. 2801 lies Thomas A. Botts--Buttons, to those who knew him.

A postcard view of Woodlawn National Cemetery around 1905. Courtesy of the Eleanor Barnes Library, Elmira, New York.

A view in Woodlawn National Cemetery.

Excerpted from
Biography Of A Rebel Prisoner:
John W. Alexander

By Hudson Alexander, great-grandnephew of John Williamson Alexander

John Williamson Alexander was born November 7, 1842 in the Pond Field community near Draytonville, South Carolina, the first child born to William Davidson Alexander and his wife, the former Miss Mary Isabella Dunn. He was named in honor of Rev. John Williamson, former minister at the Paw Creek Presbyterian Church, where the Alexander family had attended church services in Mecklenburg County, North Carolina.

During that fateful Battle of Yellow Tavern, fought out under terrible odds for the Confederate troops on May 11, 1864, John Williamson Alexander was captured by Union forces. As the battle developed, John and his brother, Rob, had become separated- which was something that had rarely happened since the two had teamed up together in the regiment. But this was no ordinary day in battle. When the dust settled, Confederate General JEB Stuart was dead, along with Colonel H.C. Pate, who commanded the Fifth Virginia Cavalry, and Captain Thomas W. Clay, who commanded Company "G" of the regiment. Brother John was marched off with the prisoners of war and, soon afterward, brother Rob rode back home in disgust - where he went back to work on the farm, never taking the oath of allegiance. In fact, he never did.

Image of John W. Alexander. Courtesy of Hudson Alexander.

John spent the next thirteen months in various Union prison camps. He was sent briefly to Fortress Monroe, then to Point Lookout and Elmira Prison in New York.

In the immediate years after the war, John Williamson Alexander was engaged in farming and was heavily involved in South Carolina politics.

The only child born to John Williamson Alexander and Sallie Tate, John Lafayette Alexander, was born on July 6, 1864 - while his father was still at Point Lookout. After the war, father and son spent a great deal of time together. And as he grew into manhood, he was told many war stories from his father's days with the Fifth Virginia.

In about 1880, most of this Alexander family left South Carolina and cast their lot with the first industrial city built from the ground up in the New South - Birmingham, Alabama. However, John remained at the old homeplace and continued to farm the ground that he had known since birth. In 1895, just months after the death of his father, John's mother became homesick for South Carolina. At that time, she moved back into the homeplace with younger brother, Jud Alexander, and John moved to another farm about a mile away. He remained there for the rest of his life.

In his latter years, John served as a magistrate in the local courts around Cherokee County, South Carolina. He was always considered a fair-minded man and a fine judge.

In 1896, sister Annie Alexander wrote to John, asking for details of his Confederate service so she could join a newly-formed organization at Gainesville, Georgia - the United Daughters of the Confederacy. In the letter he wrote back to her, he gave the dates of his service and then ended it by stating:

> "...If I done more than other true men did, or would have done, I am not aware of it. I generally went when and where ordered- and stayed until it was time to leave. The daughters of the Confederacy might make their organization a good thing, but as a rule the members of the different organizations think much more of the same than the cause they wish to perpetuate... Hope you have no trouble getting into the U.D.C....Come home during the summer, I am, Your Brother."
>
> (signed) John W. Alexander

Although we are not absolutely certain of it, the best guess of family members is that John wrote his account of life in the Union prisons at about this same time. On his original documents, written out in longhand and now in the possession of a great-great-grandson in Matthews, North Carolina, there was no date affixed to his work. Therefore, we can only speculate about when it was written.

John Williamson Alexander died June 7, 1913 in the same house where he had been born 71 years earlier at the old Alexander homeplace at Pond Field, South Carolina.

Elmira Prison Camp buildings in a 1906 postcard image of a photograph dated 1864 (probably by Moulton & Larkin). Courtesy of the Eleanor Barnes Library, Elmira, New York.

Excerpts from
Horrors Of The Damned:
A Personal Narrative Of Life In Union Prisons 1864-1865

By John W. Alexander, former prisoner of war at Elmira
Submitted by Hudson Alexander, great-grandnephew

I have been asked to write my reminiscences of thirteen months prison life at Point Lookout, Maryland, and Elmira, New York. Has it ever occurred to the reader just how little a man really knows? Oh, say, some of the books tell me so – and dare not the lines of our biographers before us. Well said – but even this, to a great extent, is secondary evidence.

Therefore, in writing these reminiscences as a private soldier at above stated prisons, I only write what a private saw and knows. "Remember, he was but an atom, a speck of dust, on the great flywheel of time; A very small cog in the mighty wheel of the '60's." He was to obey orders. He knew when he got the blow, but rarely who gae the order that caused it. Therefore, I only write what I saw and know.

A mighty responsibility rested somewhere. Those who were higher up have had little to say as to the private soldier- of his daily life, how he suffered, starved, and also how he died.

John W. Alexander
Ca. 1896

Elmira Prison

Elmira, N.Y.-- On the 17th of August we took a steamer for Baltimore, landing in this divided city. On morning of the 18th, by 10 o'clock we were halted not far from the wharf, where we stood in that August sun for two hours. Oh, how hot it was - not a breath of air. The people crowded us, and our guards as well into the middle of the street, as if it were a circus.

Butchers, fishermen, women, and their offspring crowded the better element. They stood back on the sidewalk, some of whom seemed to say by their looks, "I'm sorry." One of our best members held up some money - he wanted a little piece of tobacco. Out of all this motley throng, no one seemed to care as to his wants. Finally, a man whose arm was in a sling, was seen pushing his way through the crowd. He took the money and soon returned with the tobacco. He said he got his wound at the front two weeks before, thus proving the after told tale: the bravest are the kindest. Then, seen another - a long ganderlegged, tallow-faced specimen of the humble variety. Just as we were ready to move, he started up the street in a run and went into a house. When we got opposite, the old sinner appeared on the piazza over our heads with a huge U. S. flag, which he proceeded to wave over us. Saw another who had a large basket of ripe peaches. Soon, after we were packed in the car, a woman - God Bless her - tried to give us her fruit. The guard refused and ordered her away, but so, she got back on the embankment and threw her peaches - one at a time - over the heads of the guards and into the car.

I have been minute as to the little things and tried to portray the different characters as enabled to see them. Hence forth, there will be no laughter - no song to break the monotony. Even Lee's bad boys will say little, for we will have entered into the long night of suffering and death.

The trip [to Elmira] was uneventful, save for two boys from Lynchburg, Virginia. They cut through the back end of the car with pocket knives. The sharp crack of two rifles gave the alarm, as Ned Acre and Sam Howland dashed down the mountain side - free, free on their way to join the Holcomb Legion.

The [Elmira] prison was very much like the one we had left save for the Negroes whom we had left behind. We also missed our invalid relief. Here, the guards seemed to be a part of the climate: cold, calculating, and merciless. The only avenue to his soul was the greenback route, and this we were too poor to travel.

We were assigned tents near the outer wall and a sergeant, who had about the same power as a Captain in our Army. About four to five men were packed into a small tent, and everyone able to walk was supposed to go to the cookhouse twice a day.

The rations were about the same, bread instead of crackers. When well, a man could eat three times what he received when sick - he didn't want any of it. The water was good.

Getting acquainted here, we found many of our former comrades who had preceded us and many more that we did not know were prisoners. We also found quite a number who had signified their willingness to take the Oath of Allegiance at Point Lookout - but were still in custody.

Others with whom we came in contact with were Major Beale, the real commander inside the prison. He was an old man, whose close-fitting uniform, and skull cap formed a striking contrast to his white locks. It was before him all trespassers must appear before for their sentencing. There seemed to be no regular code of punishment. Any subordinate could put a prisoner in the guardhouse and the Major would pass the sentence. Often, a man would stay in the guardhouse for days before being taken before the Major.

The Guardhouse. This was a large structure, about 40 by 50 feet, and not until it was full of evil doers were they taken before the Major for trial- which was short and decisive. If they pleaded guilty, regardless of whether they were or not, they were discharged - otherwise, reprimanded until the house got full again.

This house was really a place of torture. Its inmates were formed into a ring each morning at half past 8, with their left hand resting on the left shoulder of his file leader. Thus, the procession started - and was kept up until half past 2.

Dinner -- no meat or soup was allowed a man in the guardhouse though this, of itself, did not matter. This was for minor offenses, such as stealing a loaf of bread or stick of wood to keep from freezing.

Just outside of the door was another circus ring. This was for the very bad men, who had stolen two loaves of bread. System and acurity meant much. Circule number two moved with the same order and time as number one, the difference being a barrel shirt and five bricks on top of it. This shirt was made out of a pork barrel by first knocking out one end, then cut a hole in the other end large enough for the head to go through. Then, get inside, stick your head through, and the bricks will hold it down- don't confuse this shirt with the cheap flour barrel shirts, which have not the weight to make them durable. So much for Major Beale and his court.

Captain Whiting. He ought to be living today for he looked in the best of health. His chief duties, so far as I could see, consisted in watching the cookhouse and the wood pile.

He was a nice little man about 35-years of age, his hair and eyes as black as night, faultlessly dressed with more buttons and uniform than Grant or Sheridan. In our army, he would have been called "Miss Nancy" or the ballroom soldier.

Of his other duties, if any, I know nothing. Truth compels me to say he performed the above written duties well.

By the 1st of October, the weather was getting cold and we began drawing wood - one stick a day to the tent. As our fireplaces were only one foot wide and the wood four feet long, we had no axe - it seemed a problem, but it was soon solved.

A light piece of sheet iron band that came around the boxes of blankets was found and put in a hastily-constructed frame, then a small file was found and a saw made from it. The price charged was one chew of tobacco for each time they sawed through our 4-foot stick, thus, it took three chews of tobacco to the stick. Then real trouble began. Someone found an old Case knife, and with this help and some wooden wedges, we were enabled to split it.

Every few days, some experts would come with crowbars and iron rods and probe into the earth beneath our tents looking for tunnels. Sometimes it snowed, and ere it was gone and we never saw the earth anymore until March. We had to police the struts every time it snowed. They have run men full while at this work, just as from over heat, and carried to their quarters where restorations were raised to bring them back to life. I could tell from the way the hearse passed our quarters that the death rate was growing. The carpenters were building our quarters for the winter, twenty feet wide and long enough to cover 135 men. Our bunks were three-deep like the shelves in a store, and two coal stoves served to keep us from freezing. The snows were heavier and 'twas fine sleighing everywhere.

The writer formed the acquaintance of an oddity on the person of the Rev. Mr. Eddy, who went about doing good. Someone said he was a Chaplain of a Texas Regiment and was captured with a gun in his hand. A Catholic - and this good man was the means of clothing hundreds, we were naked and he clothed us. Sick, and he visited us - and was all the time trying to relieve our sufferings.

I went to the dead house often, and his was the last kindly act done for our dead. After they were placed in their coffins, it was he who regulated shavings, which served for pillows for their last long sleep. This done, those rough grizzled carpenters, who were so familiar with death, formed a line with hats off while this good man repeated short burial services - the last and only service I ever heard while there. This done, the carpenters again got busy and the lids of the coffins were speedily nailed down. My recollection is that from 18 to 20 per day was an average.

January brought no relief at beating the experts. Much tunneling and planning had been done, but it remained for Judson Scruggs of now Cherokee County, S.C. to actually get out. He and two comrades started their tunnel under a house in about 35 yards of the outer wall. Only one could work at a time, so Scruggs has told me. It took six weeks, and the only tool used was a Case knife. They only worked at night, and the dirt was carried in haversacks to Chemung River. We had access to the stream at all times for sanitary reasons.

On the following morning, there was quite a stir with quick steps in every direction. Soon, we were all called out and roll of the various wards called and of a truth it was a cold time ere they found out, though the game was located- his whereabouts, never.

A word more about Captain Whiting and his troubles. The Captain was relieved, it seemed to us, of the greater part of his duties - as we were now using coal. Still he was not happy. The cookhouse must be guarded not only from the prisoners, but the rats as well. And woe be to the man that attempted to flank a ration when he was starving.

To overcome the difficulty of the rats, a man was detailed to catch them. Jim Williams, by name - never knew where Jim was from. A dog was furnished Jim for the purpose - a black bobtailed dog of medium size, with a brass collar. Jim got the meat, which he sold for five cents. I also learned that he got a premium for the scalp. The rats were very large and smelled wonderfully good when cooking. So, for a time, there was no rest at night on account of Jim and his dog around the cookhouse. Working at night in that weather and climate demanded extra food - and the dog was soon a beauty; fat and fine - and the Captain was justly pleased by his dog. Already longing eyes were being turned upon him. So poor, the boys - or the great majority- could not buy the rats. And was not the dog eating bread they ought to have? The problem was soon solved - they could eat the dog. Ere long Jim and the Captain were desolate - the source of all their joys was missing. A hurried order was issued, and everybody called out in the street until the quarters could be searched. Long after our regular evening meal, word came to disband - as they found the object of their affections. It was found in the kettles of some North Carolinians, who were promptly arrested and sent to the guard house for thirty days.

February was near now, and with it all the horrors of the damned. A man would go to bed, but could not sleep for hunger - and every half hour he would hear the sentinels cry out the time and "all's well." How it grated the souls of the starving. Finally, to relieve the agony, after he had heard that "all's well" cry at 12 o'clock and sleep refused to come, he would get up and go to some sick man, who could not eat, and borrow his ration of bread - to be paid next morning. This meant no breakfast and nothing doing in the way of eating until next evening. But, it paid - he could now sleep, and with it came the sweetest dreams mortal man was ever heir to.

He was transported at once to another climate - sometimes home, sometimes Virginia - but always where there was plenty to eat. He could see the cook bending over her duties; the coffee pot full to the brim, and in a trimble with escaping steam and see the sausage or ham and eggs - or whatever he liked best sitting on the stove. He could also hear the crackle of the fire, the coffee mill, and the rattle of the dishes - and hear the table as the cook dragged it over the floor. All was now ready - but the noise of the table had waked him.

It seemed now as if everybody was sick. Smallpox, scurvy, and chronic diarrhea were prevalent everywhere and no odds which way you turned - the scene was the same. The last load of sick was now ready to leave us, poor fellows, the majority was already in the shadow of death. Richmond Stacy and Prater Scott Montgomery, neither of which ever got home, were in this load. I.G. Sarratt also worked the rabbit foot on the doctors and left us - the parting was pathetic. No tears were shed, merely "God Bless you" was all that was said.

Among those who died now of the writer's acquaintance was: that gentle soul, Botts, familiarly called "Buttons"; William Stacy; Robert Patrick; Morgan McCombs; and Stephen Doneds - that brave Virginia boy, whom our friends in blue kept mounted. David Bailey lost five bed fellows and had to sleep by himself - the men professed to believe he was voodooed. The writer lost two - each was in dying condition ere he was taken to the hospital.

I must now descend to some matters of personal nature, which is not pleasant. The writer was taken sick with smallpox. The doctor for my ward was a young man. 'Twas Sunday morning when my condition was called to his attention. He pronounced it typhoid fever, though not fully developed - he would come again the next day. He did not come until the next Sunday, eight days, when he had me sent to smallpox hospital. I thought then - and think now - that he was more interested in checking the malady than my sufferings, which was intense. The only thing I received in the way of sustenance was cold water during those eight days - the last thing at night done for me was to fill up two canteens, 3 pints each, and place them at my head, which were invariably emptied by me during the night.

I stayed in the hospital ten days. The most important personage I met in this motley group of miserables was the "eye opener," a Texan by the name of "Hog," whose business was to open the eyes of the sufferers. Each morning the process was simple - a small pan of hot water and rag completed the ghoulish outfit. Once commenced, there was no hold up until the eyes of all were opened. One pan of water sufficed for all and when completed, the water resembled anything but water. In other respects, the treatment resembled that of the other wards and hospitals: nourishment and stimulants, plenty - after patient got too weak to receive it.

The unexpected now happened. Several months before, I had asked good friends at home to send me some tobacco - but had long ceased to look for it arriving for the delays and red tape at the exchange offices. Imagine my surprise, when informed that my name was on the bulletin board 300 yards away. Something must be done at once - to get there first was important. I was afraid to ask leave, lest my request would be refused. I also was afraid to trust anyone. Had not my good legs saved me many times when being hard pressed by our brothers in blue? True, they would not carry me as formerly, but they would at least go forward and go now - and had not my eyes been opened?

After much difficulty, I reached the coveted office - and lo and behold, there were 35 pounds of chewing tobacco awaiting me. Tobacco that sold, three for a quarter in the Southland, sold there at 75 cents per plug. For a brief period, my joy knew no bounds.

Castles were built high and fast; henceforth - I would travel the greenback route. Nourishment for the body and ease for the itching palms of those in authority still outstretched, crying "come." Yes I, too, would be free - did I not now have the key to the outer gate? Just how well I was enabled to carry out; the sequel will show.

With great effort, I succeeded in getting to my former ward with my tobacco - entirely exhausted. I had failed to discount my great weakness. My eyes were again opened to the fact that, without physical strength, I could do nothing. I could now get nourishment. This, with the kind and true comrades- and brought me back to my former condition. And with renewed strength came hope and renewed pledges to be free. I had seen many men brought in in good health from Virginia, who went away on first Truce Boat labeled "sick." But, never one who did not have a little money, or access to that of others.

It was generally conceded that the man who made out the rolls from the different hospitals meant much. He was a galvanized Southerner, said to be a native of New Orleans - and wore the badge of the traitor, the paper collar, a sure sign of the degenerate. I would see him - after another weary effort; I arrived at his office. After some maneuvering, as it were, for position. I approached him delicately as to my mission. He seemed indifferent and obdurate and, when told that I was not then in the hospital, he terminated the interview by telling me to see the doctors. I must be more explicit with this

Southern renegade. I told him I was in possession of funds which, if I could get out, I would not need - and would cheerfully leave it to those who would assist me. His whole demeanor changed - he now spoke kindly, but when told that my stock in trade was tobacco, he reminded me that the long green would be better. Where upon, I asked the amount - and he said five dollars.

Then, he would have me sent to the hospital that he was then making up the next load of sick. The money was to be paid after I got to the hospital, and my name was on the roll. Expectations ran high. It seemed as if I could already feel the loosening of my fetters. A dream never to be realized. The next morning found me again in wonderland, half-delirious. The exertion had proved too much for my poor strength, and I must pay the penalty.

Days passed now, of which I knew but little. But, my stupor was to have a rude awakening. In the dead of night my reasoning returned, only to hear the rattle of countless hammering and hand saws at work. The ice and snow were melting. Chemung River was breaking all bounds - already a portion of the prison was washed away. The "all's well" of the guard, for once, was silent. The murmur of many voices could now be heard, coupled with the carpenters at work. It was evident that all was not well. By daylight (March 16-17, 1865), the water was everywhere- and as fast as boats could be finished and manned, the work of rescue commenced. By 12 o'clock, a boat was paddled into my door and I was laid gently into it, and I was ferried outside where tents were provided.

Rumor said forty of our poor fellows died that night - and all agreed that Major Beale and officers did their best to protect the sick. As the water in cookhouse was threatening to wash it away, Captain Whiting's charity came to the surface and those inclined to sick were told they could have what they wanted. This was considerable in the way of barrels of flour and pork. We didn't give the Captain much credit for his charity, as 'twas the old tale of giving to the poor folks what you can't use yourself.

It was now the last days of March, when I was sent to the hospital for good- but this time, conditions were better. My doctor, Williams of Maine, was a man to know, who kept me with him until released. Few men could have been so kind, and none could have been better. A true Republican, but an honest man.

Thus was all my dreams of an early release shattered. The railroads were washed out, which caused delays. Then came Appomattox, and Mr. Lincoln's death soon after made it plain that boat loads of sick were a thing of the past. I never saw this Southern vampire again. I had my tobacco and the money.

Dr. Williams saw me twice each day, and saw to it that I was treated ok. At one time, he brought two other doctors with him to consult over my case - and when I, at last, was able to walk about, the medical director of the prison ordered me back to my ward, Dr. Williams stoutly refused and kept me with him. So kind and true was this good man to me, that I would gladly have exchanged some of my would-be Southern friends for more like him.

During this time, I saw and heard little from camp, save what my good friend David Bailey told me. He came to see me often, and the boys in my former ward said 'twas bad omen - and I would go the way of the five bed fellows heretofore mentioned.

The money went fast. I could buy a good U.S. blanket for 25-cents; a good pair of brogan shoes for 25-cents; a pint of whiskey for 25-cents; a pint of milk punch for 5-cents; a good shirt for 15-cents; and a pint of beans with soup strained out for 5-cents. The reason for this was that Ward Sergeants, Sick Sergeants, Dispensary Clerks, and many who had the opportunity - were stealing from the Government. Besides, there were hundreds on detail, for one excuse or another, who wore the paper collar. They were called galvanized -- a term used to distinguish them from their Southern brothers. Who was responsible for all this, I never knew. Did the Government make an allowance for this state of affairs? Or did the prisoners? I never knew all this, but I did know that we were starving in a land of plenty.

Release From Prison

On the 23rd of June, I was released and arrived in New York on the following morning - and was treated kindly by all whom I met, save for a few who had been too cowardly to go to the front.

After a rest of three days, we went aboard the steamer "Anaga," bound for Hilton Head, South Carolina. Of the trip but little remains to be told, although we had taken an oath to support the Constitution of the U. S. against all enemies, either foreign or domestic. We were still prisoners, if not in war- in fact. We were huddled together about the middle of the upper deck of the vessel. Behind us was the quarter deck, where none but first-class passengers were allowed; in front was about fifty steers going to feed the hungry at Hilton Head.

Our allowance was hard bread and salted beef, along with one quart of condensed water per day. It was so hot you could, with difficulty, hold it in your hand. This water was caught from the drippings from machinery. Salted beef, hard tack, and a July sun did not allay our thirst. First-class passengers had all the ice water needed. The steers had all the fresh they would drink. Why should we perish? Were we not the third class?

There were four life boats corded securely to the side of the vessel- in each was a ten-gallon keg of water. The intention, no doubt, was to have this water in case of accidents or emergency. Had not the emergency arrived? A box lid was procured and two pieces made as near a joint as possible. Then a small groove was cut in one of them. A small twine and piece of old newspaper were all that was needed. Daylight was used to make it- and soon after dark we crawled carefully over the side of the vessel into the life boat. The balance was easy. The spigot, once out, left nothing to do but lie down and get busy with the ill-improvised need. It worked well, and ere daylight dawned, the four kegs were empty. Besides getting the water, 'twas satisfaction to know that - in case of a disaster - all would fare alike.

Some four days after leaving New York we arrived at Hilton Head- here we changed vessels as the "Anaga" could not cross the bar at Charleston.

On the next evening we arrived in Charleston Harbor. We were soon put ashore and marched to a large brick building on the southern wharf. Our escort now left us for good - we were at last free. We had become so used to looking to others for food, that we looked in vain for someone to come with rations. The contrast was great between this greeting and the one accorded us when we were in the city in the early days of the war.

My friend, Pickney Garner, got a small musk mellon, which served for supper and breakfast. He reported seeing no white people. Others went to the South Carolina depot and reported that the railroad people would take us to Orangeburg - provided we would ride on the top of the cars. This would be better than walking - and the offer was gladly accepted. By sunrise the next morning, we were at the depot. The sick were kindly helped to the best places by their comrades and we were soon on our way to the up country.

We arrived at Orangeburg at about 4 o'clock p.m. The ride on the tin roof cars, in that July sun, was not pleasant. Here, we divided into units and walked to Columbia. 'Twas an effort of the survival, of the few once again.

I have omitted to make any mention of my enfeebled condition- and after going four miles, I found myself exhausted. Bidding my comrades to leave me, which they did with reluctance, I laid down on mother earth to rest. I had no blanket, but I could rest. In about an hour or two, I saw a light on a nearby mound. I must have water. I went at once to the light and got a canteen of water. This was all he had - Sherman had been there and scared all the life out of him. When I reminded him that I had not eaten anything since the day before, he kindly gave me a glass of milk to be taken from his piazza. He was afraid of smallpox. He could not allow me in his house. Poor man, he was too cowardly for his day and generation.

I rested well - no time was lost. By the break of day, I was on my way - no time was consumed with breakfast or beds. An empty haversack and canteen constituted my earthly belongings. My tramp would not be impeded by our weight. But, I was not to make my journey all alone- half a mile up the road; I spied a solitary figure who seemed in the distance to be more drunk than otherwise. So much did he reil and waver as he walked from weakness. I soon overtook him and found out that he lived in Chester, South Carolina. Like me, he was using every effort to get home. His name was Samuel Micke. Hence forth, we were to be partners; neither could out-walk the other. To write all the details of our trip to Columbia would make this article too long.

On the sixth or seventh day, Micke and myself arrived in Columbia. Sherman had destroyed everything along the way. All the best houses were burnt, and people gone, and those remaining were starving. Lone chimneys and dead shade trees told the tale.

We could only travel about five or six miles a day - and we stayed on

Sherman's trail all the way, and lived off fruit and corn. The few white people seen were in such object poverty that we did not bother them. Traveling Sherman's Trail had been depressing, but imagine our feelings when we halted to rest opposite Janney's Hotel (the Congaree Hotel owned by J.C. Janney, which was located on the west side of Washington Street in Columbia). This had been the Mecca for the up country. Many had rested here - the true and the brave were always welcome. No friendly greeting to the foot sore and weary. The trees and blackened walls told the tale. It seemed to us that none, but a monster of cruelty could have done this.

After a short rest, Micke and I split up. The only sign of life was a large tent down by the depot. 'Twas a commissary, and I was soon at its door. The officer inside eyed me critically. Upon being told that I was a paroled prisoner and still 90 miles from home, he informed me that his instructions did not authorize him to give me anything. Then, with some of the choicest adjectives, said he would give me what I wanted. I got nine pounds of flour, four pounds of bacon, one pound ground coffee, and one pound of sugar. An old Negro woman converted my flour into bread - and I had my first cup of coffee I had tasted in 14 months. And I was grateful to my brothers in Blue.

I was restored to family in the up country on the 12th of July, 1865.

A quiet day at Woodlawn National Cemetery.

Calvin Hathcock, 42 NCT

Submitted by Art Hathcock, great-great-great grandson

Have nothing else other than his cousin Irvin Anderson Hathcock being a Sergeant in Co. H of the 42nd North Carolina Troops. Calvin was from the 42nd NCT. Irvin was my great-great-great uncle and went on to be a medical doctor. The family during the Civil War lived on the waters of Little Meadow Creek (Reeds Gold Mine Creek) and had a bunch of land. Our family runs deep in North Carolina and I am very proud of my name.

My great-great-great grandfather was a gold miner and was listed in the Confederate government as "occupation: gold miner." Most all of the family were musicians, as Calvin was. They made money playing music at weddings, etc. They had plenty of money at that time due to land grants from England prior to the Revolution, and business dealings. The old family home site area is near what is now Locust, North Carolina. They never owned slaves, and most of the family was cautious about the government split, but when the split occurred , they traveled long distances to enlist in the Confederate government. Hence, the family being in multiple regiments. I think there is about five different regiments, not sure though. My great-great-great grandfather was almost killed at Gettysburg, and again at Fisher's Hill on August 13, 1864. It is sad that Calvin died in the Elmira prison. If I am not mistaken, he was the only one to die from the family during the Civil War. Through my research and opinion, all prisons during the Civil War were very bad, and just as bad as the South. In fact, my opinion is more so because the North had plenty of food and clothing and did nothing to help its prisoners unlike the South. I hope you honor these young soldiers that were far away from home that never returned... The 28th NCT/Lanes Brigade were last to leave the wall at Gettysburg. Heavily honored Confederate Regiment all the way to the end.

List of Confederate Dead in Woodlawn National Cemetery, Elmira, New York

Name	Date of Death	State	Company	Regiment/Notes	Woodlawn
ABEL, C.T.	November 5, 1864	Virginia	H	4th Cavalry	836
ABERNATHY, F.D.	August 6, 1864	North Carolina	B	2nd Cavalry	141
ADAIR, W.H.	May 18, 1865	Alabama	E	10th	2946
ADAMS, A.	February 17, 1865	South Carolina	H	25th	2219
ADAMS, E.C.	February 11, 1865	Virginia	B	50th	2083
ADAMS, J.W.	March 10, 1865	Georgia	C	24th	1548
ADAMS, James	December 19, 1864	Alabama	E	1st Battalion of Artillery	1734
ADAMS, John	October 6, 1864	North Carolina	D	3rd	591
ADAMS, John	November 21, 1864	Alabama	A	21st	942
ADAMS, John	October 10, 1864	Georgia	A	38th	687
ADAMS, Joseph	July 15, 1864	North Carolina	A	51st	Shohola
ADAMS, L.H.	February 20, 1865	Georgia	B	16th	2312
ADAMS, R.W.	January 3, 1865	South Carolina	B	4th Cavalry	1267
ADAMS, Samuel	February 28, 1865	Louisiana	B	5th	2135
ADAMS, William	September 18, 1864	North Carolina	K	30th	514
ADAMS, William B.	March 3, 1865	Virginia	D	44th	1816
ADAMS, William S.	December 7, 1864	Alabama	E	1st Battalion of Artillery	1293
ADCOCK, Green	October 4, 1864	Tennessee	G	25th	652
ADKINS, William H.	January 15, 1865	North Carolina	K	30th	1450
AGEE, Charles	February 19, 1865	Virginia	H	42nd	2325
AGERTON, John	December 11, 1864	Georgia	D	48th	1058
AIKEN, Malachan	April 5, 1865	Georgia	C	2nd	2626
AKENS, D.W.	September 17, 1864	Georgia	B	7th Cavalry	170

Name	Date of Death	State	Company	Regiment/Notes	Woodlawn
ALDERMAN, A.C.	November 27, 1864	Virginia	I	25th - Corporal	901
ALDERMAN, I.E.	December 20, 1864	Georgia	C	61st	1074
ALDRIDGE, Ransom	March 3, 1865	North Carolina	H	3rd	2013
ALEXANDER, John	November 18, 1864	Virginia	D	25th	966
ALEXANDER, Thomas A.	August 11, 1864	North Carolina	E	37th	134
ALEXANDER, W.H.	September 20, 1864	North Carolina	F	32nd	333
ALFORD, Josiah	October 24, 1864	North Carolina	I	1st	861
ALGERS, Isaac H.	April 11, 1865	Alabama	F	1st Battalion of Artillery	2697
ALL, William	January 3, 1865	Georgia	D	44th	1266
ALLBRIGHT, John	October 1, 1864	North Carolina	H	1st	403
ALLEN, Alexander T.	February 1, 1865	North Carolina	F	2nd Cavalry	1762
ALLEN, Barton H.	October 16, 1864	Virginia	H	5th	559
ALLEN, David J.	December 22, 1864	Louisiana	D	9th Cavalry	1089
ALLEN, Drury	February 20, 1865	South Carolina	E	25th	2308
ALLEN, J.L.	September 27, 1864	Virginia	G	6th Cavalry	388
ALLEN, John R. B.	April 19, 1865	Alabama	E	1st Battalion of Artillery	1368
ALLEN, Richard B.	December 13, 1864	Alabama	K	59th	1122
ALLEN, Thomas	February 8, 1865	Alabama	E	1st Battalion of Artillery	1934
ALLEN, Thomas C.	February 10, 1865	Alabama	C	1st Artillery	2092
ALLEN, Thomas T.	February 19, 1865	North Carolina	F	36th	2327
ALLEY, John	February 26, 1865	Florida	A	1st Reserve	2298
ALLEY, Thomas K.	September 19, 1864	Virginia	A	1st Artillery	320
ALLISON, Humphrey D.	October 28, 1864	Florida	B	5th - Sergeant	719
ALMOND, J.W.	May 18, 1865	Georgia	D	3rd	2952

Name	Date of Death	State	Company	Regiment/Notes	Woodlawn
ALSOM, Floyd	November 20, 1864	Virginia	K	2nd Cavalry	932
ALTMAN, James P.	March 29, 1865	South Carolina	A	21st	2536
ALTMAN, Nathan	April 18, 1865	North Carolina	G	40th	1361
ALTMAN, JAMES, A.	August 3, 1864	Virginia		Citizen of Virginia	5
ANDERSON, G.H.	April 10, 1865	North Carolina	D	36th Artillery	2674
ANDERSON, G.W.	January 3, 1865	Virginia	D	26th	1476
ANDERSON, George	September 18, 1864	North Carolina	G	8th	152
ANDERSON, George W.	October 9, 1864	Virginia	E	25th	673
ANDERSON, J.W.	October 19, 1864	Virginia	C	3rd Cavalry	537
ANDERSON, James P.	October 12, 1865	Georgia	I	61st	2043
ANDERSON, John M.	October 7, 1864	Georgia	C	Cobb's Legion	586
ANDERSON, Richard	January 26, 1865	North Carolin	D	7th	1630
ANDERSON, Robert	January 16, 1865	Virginia	A	42nd	1439
ANDREWS, J.J.D.	April 10, 1865	North Carolina	F	31st Sergeant	2662
ANDREWS, John W.	September 19, 1864	Virginia	A	21st	322
ANDREWS, William C.	November 21, 1864	North Carolina	D	18th – Corporal	974
ANDREWS, William W.	December 26, 1864	Alabama	I	13th	1288
ANTHONY, John	October 26, 1864	North Carolina	D	1st	715
ANTHONY, Miskel	December 13, 1864	Virginia	I	40th	1129
ANTON, J.C.	March 13, 1865	North Carolina	D	5th	1727
ARD, Benjamin	June 1, 1865	South Carolina	I	25th – Corporal	2904
ARD, E.H.	September 20, 1864	South Carolina	K	21st	340
ARMAND, E.	March 28, 1865	Louisiana	E	2nd	2496

Name	Date of Death	State	Company	Regiment/Notes	Woodlawn
ARMSTRONG, Henry W.	December 7, 1864	North Carolina	C	18th	1176
ARMSTRONG, Joseph A.	September 14, 1864	Virginia	F	25th	273
ARMSTRONG, Price O.F.	August 24, 1864	Virginia	D	44th	40
ARMSTRONG, R.C.	January 28, 1865	Texas	I	4th	1811
ARRINGTON, James L.	February 7, 1865	North Carolina	B	30th	1925
ARWOOD, David	March 3, 1865	North Carolina	D	13th	1815
ASHCROFT, S.H.	September 9, 1864	Virginia	A	48th	208
ASKEW, Thomas	December 13, 1864	North Carolina	H	1st - Corporal	1132
ASTON, L.	December 3, 1864	North Carolina	A	51st	880
ATKINS, Wiley	January 6, 1865	North Carolina	K	1st	1246
ATKINSON, M.W.	March 1, 1865	Virginia	I	59th - Corporal	2110
ATKINSON, Thomas	April 6, 1865	South Carolina	G	21st	2631
AUSTIN, J.W.	September 3, 1864	North Carolina	F	32nd	60
AUSTIN, Richard	June 11, 1865	North Carolina	C	3rd Battalion	2886
AUSTIN, S.S.	December 11, 1864	North Carolina	C, K	28th	1148
AUSTIN, T.J.	July 7, 1865	Alabama	A	21st	2839
AUTERY, Micajah	April 9, 1865	North Carolina	C	36th	2621
AUTRY, Isaac B.	May 23, 1865	North Carolina	F	24th	2931
AUTRY, James C.	November 16, 1864	North Carolina	F	32nd	802
AUTRY, Miles C.	October 24, 1864	North Carolina	F	24th - Sergeant	859
AVANT, S.	September 26, 1864	South Carolina	E	27th - Sergeant	447
AVENT, John	December 12, 1864	Virginia		Citizen of Virginia	1146
AYRE, Richard T.	February 17, 1865	North Carolina	C	23rd	2220
BAILEY, Charles	April 19, 1865	South Carolina	G	25th	1377

Name	Date of Death	State	Company	Regiment/Notes	Woodlawn
BAILEY, D.T.	December 9, 1864	Virginia	E	20th Cavalry	1163
BAILEY, Elias D.	February 19, 1865	North Carolina	K	3rd	2353
BAILEY, H.L.	March 5, 1865	South Carolina	G	25th	2426
BAILEY, H.M.	February 13, 1865	Georgia	C	16th	2039
BAILEY, John B.	March 19, 1865	South Carolina	I	11th	1726
BAIN, Daniel B.	October 27, 1864	North Carolina	F	24th	714
BAIN, Samuel O.	February 24, 1865	North Carolina	F	10th Artillery	2258
BAIRD, James H.	August 28, 1864	North Carolina	C	18th	50
BAISDEN, K.H.	April 5, 1865	North Carolina	K	51st	2551
BAKER, J.	May 4, 1865	Virginia	E	26th	2757
BAKER, James A.	March 14, 1865	North Carolina	C	36th, 2nd Artillery	1666
BAKER, Jesse E.	July 15, 1864	North Carolina	F	51st	Shohola
BAKER, M.A.D.	March 31, 1865	South Carolina	C	25th Reserve	2601
BALDWIN, R.W.	December 10, 1864	Tennessee	H	63rd	1054
BALL, Levi	March 18, 1865	North Carolina	H	44th	1720
BALANCE, Holoway	November 7, 1864	North Carolina	H	33rd	772
BALLARD, Archibald	January 6, 1865	Virginia	H	26th Sergeant	1504
BANKS, Amos	February 12, 1865	Georgia	H	7th Cavalry	2077
BANKS, George W.	August 2, 1864	Virginia	D	9th	146
BANKS, Robert R.	October 17, 1864	Alabama	C	4th	541
BANKSTON, Joseph C.	November 24, 1864	Alabama	I	3rd Corporal	919
BANNINGER, M.	September 24, 1864	North Carolina	B	5th	336
BARBER, J.	May 12, 1865	Georgia	I	14th	2798
BARBER, J.D.	June 26, 1865	South Carolina	F	25th	2823

Name	Date of Death	State	Company	Regiment/Notes	Woodlawn
BARBER, J.J.	November 18, 1864	North Carolina	H	12th - Sergeant	971
BARBER, W.R.	March 29, 1865	North Carolina	E	3rd - State Troop	2539
BARCO, Willoughby	January 13, 1865	North Carolina	B	8th	1489
BARKER, Joshua	February 9, 1865	South Carolina	A	1st - Rifles	1949
BARKER, Quentin	February 6, 1865	North Carolina	G	1st -Corporal-State Troop	2212
BARLOW, Jesse F.	May 15, 1865	Alabama	E	1st Battalion of Artillery	2807
BARLOW, William R.	January 31, 1865	North Carolina	B	18th	1787
*BARMAN, Jonas	September 12, 1864	North Carolina	B	31st	177
BARNARD, Richard J.	September 22, 1864	Virginia	K	50th	487
BARNES, Aldridge A.	October 4, 1864	North Carolina	E	51st	640
BARNES, C.C.	April 23, 1865	North Carolina	B	40th	1400
BARNES, C.M.	February 17, 1865	Georgia	G	46th	2197
BARNES, D.F.	December 15, 1864	North Carolina	D	22nd	1016
BARNES, Edmund	April 3, 1865	Virginia	E	59th	2568
BARNES, F.H.	April 1, 1865	South Carolina	I	25th	2587
BARNES, Francis	October 5, 1864	North Carolina	A	32nd	642
BARNES, S.M.	March 7, 1865	Alabama	F	1st Battalion of Artillery	1958
BARNES, Z.	September 11, 1864	Louisiana	H	10th - Corporal	253
BARNETT, A.B.	March 9, 1865	North Carolina	G	36th	2371
BARNETT, Henry H.	March 12, 1865	Alabama	C	1st Battalion of Artillery	1831
BARNHART, B.	May 31, 1865	Virginia	F	22nd	2906
*BARNHILL, D.R.	March 9, 1865	North Carolina	H	36th	1878
BARRETT, Laban	September 14, 1864	Georgia	K	14th	288

Woodlawn National Cemetery is located at 1825 Davis Street in Elmira, New York 14901. Nearby, also on Davis Street, is the John W. Jones Museum. Mr. Jones was a runaway slave from Virginia who found comfort and safety in Elmira. He was the sexton of the cemetery and kept the records of the deceased soldiers. His primary job was to see that every soldier had a proper burial.

Name	Date of Death	State	Company	Regiment/Notes	Woodlawn
BARRICK, Milton	February 12, 1865	Georgia	E	3rd - Corporal	2031
BARRIER, John A.	January 14, 1865	North Carolina	H	8th	1462
BARRIER, L.C.	March 23, 1865	North Carolina	H	8th	1509
BARRING, A.	May 1, 1865	North Carolina	K	8th	2739
BARRINGER, A.C.	February 15, 1865	North Carolina	F	5th	2193
BARRINGTON, Lander	March 24, 1865	North Carolina	K	40th	2453
BARRON, J.	May 2, 1865	North Carolina	D	40th	2746
BARTHOLOMEW, I.W.	September 3, 1864	North Carolina	K	12th	225
BARTLETT, Fred	October 26, 1864	Louisiana	F	10th	624
BARWICK, John	January 13, 1865	Georgia	F	64th	1477
BASDIN, Jackson	September 27, 1864	North Carolina	B	66th	386
BASHAM, W.H.	October 16, 1864	Virginia	F	26th	556
BASS, Benjamin	January 17, 1865	North Carolina	H	45th	1443
BASS, Cornelius	May 24, 1865	North Carolina	E	40th, 3rd Artillery-State Troop	2924
BASS, George	March 24, 1865	North Carolina	H	32nd	1508
BATES, Nathan S.	September 9, 1864	Georgia	I	19th	1194
BAUCUM, Thomas	December 1, 1864	North Carolina	E	33rd	1012
BAXLEY, John W.	July 15, 1864	North Carolina	A	31st	Shohola
BAXLEY, Joseph	January 29, 1865	Georgia	H	9th	1804
BAXTER, George H.	January 9, 1865	Virginia	C	25th	1222
BAYLESS, A.J.	October 21, 1864	Alabama	A	21st	527
BEACH, Rizon	March 4, 1865	Virginia	A	49th	1982
BEACHUM, James A.	February 13, 1865	North Carolina	K	43rd	2069

Name	Date of Death	State	Company	Regiment/Notes	Woodlawn
BEACHUM, Joseph J.	January 25, 1865	North Carolina	K	43rd	1616
BEALL, Albert B.	February 25, 1865	Georgia	B	12th	2311
BEALS, Amos	August 13, 1864	Tennessee	D	7th	17
BEAMER, J.W.	March 8, 1865	Virginia	F	2nd	2383
BEAN, Alexander	January 5, 1865	North Carolina	K	5th	1237
BEAN, Benjamin F.	December 7, 1864	North Carolina	I	5th	1178
BEAREN, E.M.	March 28, 1865	North Carolina	K	5th	2504
BEASON, J.T.	May 20, 1865	Alabama	F	1st Battalion of Artillery	2943
*BEATTY, C.B.	February 24, 1865	South Carolina	A	18th	2255
BEATTY, Jonathan P.	November 26, 1864	North Carolina	B	28th	907
BEAUCHAMP, J.S.	February 10, 1865	Louisiana	E	6th Cavalry	2089
BECK, W.S.	October 12, 1864	Georgia	K	59th	567
BECKERDITE, P.F.	October 4, 1864	North Carolina		Citizen of North Carolina	613
BECKNER, S.B.	August 2, 1864	Virginia	I	26th	4
BEHELER, J.	September 1, 1864	South Carolina	F	17th	77
BELCHER, William	November 28, 1864	Georgia	B	7th Cavalry	983
BELL, F.C.	October 24, 1864	Georgia	E	7th Cavalry	852
BELL, John	May 3, 1865	Florida	H	8th	2751
BELL, John S.	October 17, 1864	Virginia	I	50th	551
BELLAMY, Richard C.	November 27, 1864	Florida	A	5th	903
BELLOTTE, J.D.	March 16, 1865	South Carolina	C	4th Cavalry	1700
BELTON, James R.	March 11, 1865	North Carolina	A	28th	1869
BELTON, Thornton	February 6, 1865	North Carolina	F	45th	1911

Name	Date of Death	State	Company	Regiment/Notes	Woodlawn
*BENFIELD, R.A.	February 25, 1865	North Carolina	I	52nd	2284
BENN, William R.	April 12, 1865	Virginia	E	7th Cavalry	1389
BENNETT, A.J.	January 25, 1865	North Carolina	E	45th	1626
BENNETT, Albert A.	February 13, 1865	Georgia	B	12th	2037
BENNETT, Christian G.	September 23, 1864	Georgia	B	20th	356
BENNETT, G.P.	July 26, 1865	Georgia	G	15th	2862
BENNETT, John H.	June 1, 1865	North Carolina	F	21st	2905
BENNETT, Samuel H.	December 12, 1864	Virginia	E	38th	1087
BENNIFIELD, David	February 20, 1865	Alabama	F	1st Battalion of Artillery	2309
BENTON, Josh	October 1, 1864	South Carolina	I	11th	419
*BENTON, Theodore	December 10, 1864	Louisiana	B	1st	1158
BEOFFORD, Wesley	April 10, 1865	North Carolina	H	10th	2671
BERRY, Benjamin B.	December 27, 1864	Tennessee	I	14th	898
BERRY, Charles W.	July 8, 1865	Virginia	G	25th - Sergeant	2841
BERRY, John	September 24, 1864	Virginia	F	15th Cavalry - Sergeant	367
BERRYHILL, Alfred	February 10, 1865	Alabama	E	1st Battalion of Artillery	2095
BERTRAM, William E.	September 21, 1864	Tennessee	D	25th	351
BESSENT, J.H.	July 15, 1864	North Carolina	G	51st - Corporal	Shohola
BEST, Archibald	September 11, 1864	Florida	H	11th	258
BETTS, J.H.	January 27, 1865	Georgia	I	16th - Sergeant	1651
BEVERLY, John,	February 27, 1865	South Carolina	D	25th	2123
BIBBS, D.L.	September 24, 1864	Virginia	K	50th	472
BIDDLE, George W.	March 4, 1865	Virginia	I	53rd	2000

Name	Date of Death	State	Company	Regiment/Notes	Woodlawn
BIGGS, Jefferson	March 30, 1865	North Carolina	G	36th	2590
BIRD, B.	November 12, 1864	Florida	L	11th	936
BIRD, B.	February 17, 1865	Virginia	D	17th Cavalry	2225
BIRD, J.H.	July 15, 1864	Virginia	I	26th	Shohola
BIRD, Matthew	March 28, 1865	South Carolina	G	21st	2508
BISHOP, J.W.	December 13, 1864	North Carolina	B	32nd	1126
BISHOP, James	November 9, 1864	South Carolina	D	17th	784
BITER, John	October 10, 1864	South Carolina	C	22nd Cavalry	664
BLACK, Daniel L.	September 26, 1864	South Carolina	G	4th	377
BLACK, E.M.	November 7, 1864	North Carolina	K	45th	777
BLACK, John D.	October 9, 1864	Virginia	I	50th	653
BLACK, Willis	April 19, 1865	Alabama	G	12th	1372
BLACKBURN, James T.	September 13, 1864	North Carolina	A	34th	274
BLACKBURN, Kennon	February 28, 1865	North Carolina	I	36th	2116
BLACKBURN, M.E.L.	November 3, 1864	Georgia	G	7th Cavalry	841
BLACKMAN, James	March 6, 1865	South Carolina	B	21st	2416
BLACKMAN, R.A.	June 3, 1865	North Carolina	A	36th	2899
BLACKWELL, John O.	November 12, 1864	Virginia	H	40th	973
BLACKWELL, Samuel	February 3, 1865	South Carolina	B	6th Cavalry	1752
BLACKWOOD, John K.	December 14, 1864	South Carolina	K	Holcombe Legion	1118
BLACKWOOD, Joseph	March 3, 1865	North Carolina	H	37th	1993
BLAIR, William C.	October 9, 1864	Alabama	C	12th	657
BLAKE, Robert	February 27, 1865	North Carolina	G	40th	2129

Name	Date of Death	State	Company	Regiment/Notes	Woodlawn
BLAND, John	September 19, 1864	North Carolina	I	18th	518
BLANTON, J.J.	January 18, 1865	North Carolina	G	51st	1431
*BLANTON, W.J.	October 10, 1864	North Carolina	A	49th	662
BLARNEY, John	December 25, 1864	Florida	H	Reserves	1114
BLAYLOCK, Albert	September 11, 1864	North Carolina	E	35th	257
BLAYLOCK, Calvin	March 29, 1865	North Carolina	H	14th	2506
BLIZZARD, John D.	December 4, 1864	North Carolina	B	56th	882
BLOODWORTH, J.H.	January 26, 1865	Alabama	G	5th	1635
BLYTHE, L.W.	September 20, 1864	North Carolina	I	37th	498
BOEHUR, W.H.	September 9, 1864	Virginia		Imboden's Brigade, Signal Guard	209
BOGAN, Benjamin I.	December 9, 1864	South Carolina	H	1st	1160
BOGGS, William	December 19, 1864	Virginia	E	26th	1071
BOGLE, G.W.	August 23, 1864	North Carolina	H	56th	42
*BOIE, Mitchell	January 23, 1865	North Carolina	K	18th	1594
BOLDEN, Calvin	September 30, 1864	North Carolina	B	28th	398
*BOLES, Richard	November 4, 1864	Alabama	B	13th - Southern Stars	842
BOND, J.F.	February 18, 1865	North Carolina	K	10th	2349
BONEY, John B.	January 8, 1865	North Carolina	G	61st	1499
BOONE, Sampson	November 24, 1864	North Carolina	G	51st	913
BOONE, Thomas E.	September 20, 1864	Virginia	C	25th	352
BOOTH, Cornelius	October 12, 1864	Virginia	B	42nd	571
BOSHEN, A.A.	September 16, 1864	North Carolina	K	5th	302
BOSTICK, A.H.	July 4, 1865	Virginia	C	26th	2836

Elmira Prison Camp

Name	Date of Death	State	Company	Regiment/Notes	Woodlawn
BOSTICK, Henry J.	January 14, 1865	Georgia	I	12th	1464
BOSWELL, Hamilton L.	January 3, 1865	Tennessee	D	25th - Corporal	1259
BOSWELL, James C.	September 23, 1864	Virginia	C	39th Battalion Cavalry	474
*BOTTS, F.A.	May 4, 1865	South Carolina		Holcombe Legion	2801
BOUGHTON, Thomas	November 11, 1864	Virginia	C	26th	788
BOURNE, J.	May 10, 1865	Virginia	H	5th	2785
BOWEN, Lawrence	September 21, 1864	North Carolina	H	1st	348
BOWEN, William H.	October 22, 1864	Georgia	G	49th	869
BOWERS, A.	March 7, 1865	South Carolina	H	22nd - Sergeant	2395
BOWERS, Joseph	September 4, 1864	Virginia	C	29th	231
BOWERS, W.	July 15, 1864	North Carolina	B	48th	Shohola
BOWIE, W.P.	September 2, 1864	Louisiana	A	22nd	62
BOWLES, N.A.	November 29, 1864	Georgia	C	7th	992
BOWLIN, Danile A.	April 2, 1865	Georgia	F	21st	2582
BOWLING, John W.	January 11, 1865	Virginia	C	50th - Sergeant	1494
BOWMAN, Madison	September 1, 1864	Virginia	K	21st Cavalry	90
BOWMAN, W.H.	February 12, 1865	Mississippi		Citizen of Mississippi	2050
BOYD, Enoch	December 29, 1864	Alabama	C	1st Battalion of Artillery	1309
BOYD, John	February 5, 1865	Alabama	F	1st Battalion of Artillery	1894
BOYER, Jacob	February 5, 1865	North Carolina	B	5th	1740
BRADBERRY, J.H.	April 13, 1865	Alabama	C	5th	2678
BRADNOR, James A.	October 9, 1864	Virginia	D	39th Battalion	663
BRADY, H.H.	February 21, 1865	North Carolina	F	36th	2313
BRADY, T.J.	June 6, 1865	Georgia	D	16th	2891

Name	Date of Death	State	Company	Regiment/Notes	Woodlawn
BRAFFORD, Joshua	April 21, 1865	North Carolina	F	10th	1392
BRAND, A.R.	January 4, 1865	Confederate States Navy "Bombshell" Fireman, Sailor			1263
BRANDENBURG, John	February 9, 1865	Louisiana	K	7th	1940
BRANNON, Hugh	September 7, 1864	South Carolina	H	18th	219
BRANNON, J.F.	March 30, 1865	Georgia	K	35th	2520
BRANNON, R.H.	November 28, 1864	Florida	H	6th	984
BRANTON, H.H.	November 24, 1864	North Carolina	I	3rd	911
BRANTON, John	February 2, 1865	Virginia	E	59th	1758
BRASSWELL, Sidney	March 9, 1865	North Carolina	H	32nd	2367
BRAY, J.R.	September 21, 1864	Virginia	E	5th Cavalry	334
BRAYLESS, J.	September 26, 1864	Virginia	H	26th	448
BRECKENRIDGE, Joseph F.	March 23, 1865	Alabama	I	61st	1671
BREEDEN, James	November 14, 1864	Tennessee	B	1st	805
BREEDING, James L.	November 26, 1864	Virginia	I	50th	906
BREWER, Wiley	November 15, 1864	North Carolina	A	3rd	806
BREWSTER, William D.	October 16, 1864	Georgia	D	6th	548
BRICKETT, J.H.	June 15, 1865	South Carolina	H	25th - Sergeant	2880
BRIGGS, R.	July 15, 1864	North Carolina	E	31st	Shohola
BRIGHT, J.W.	July 15, 1864	Virginia	A	26th	Shohola
BRIGHT, Jonathan	September 12, 1864	North Carolina	I	8th	250
BRIGHT, Robert B.	September 13, 1864	South Carolina	H	22nd	262
BRIGHT, Samuel S.	March 2, 1865	North Carolina	B	36th	2008
BRIGHT, W.J.	September 23, 1864	South Carolina	C	22nd	469

Name	Date of Death	State	Company	Regiment/Notes	Woodlawn
BRIMM, R.	November 11, 1864	North Carolina	G	45t	793
*BRINKLEY, Fetherd	November 26, 1864	North Carolina	E	33rd	908
BRINKLEY, William	September 28, 1864	North Carolina	I	33rd	396
BRINSGER, W.H.	August 24, 1864	North Carolina	H	5th	39
BRINSON, F.W.	March 3, 1865	North Carolina	B	3rd	1519
BRINSON, J.L.	December 11, 1864	Georgia	B	7th Sergeant	1049
BRISTOW, Daniel	March 3, 1865	South Carolina	F	21st	1998
BRISTOW, J.A.	April 1, 1865	North Carolina	F	1st	2653
BRISTOW, James T.	October 10, 1864	Virginia	B	26th	671
BRISTOW, R.N.	March 18, 1865	South Carolina	F	21st	1719
BRITT, W.F.	October 5, 1864	Virginia	B	48th	604
BRITTE, Ellis	September 28, 1864	North Carolina	D	18th - Corporal	428
BRITTON, W.J.	March 2, 1865	Georgia	D	Cobb's Legion	2019
BROADWAY, David T.	February 6, 1865	North Carolina	A	54th	1914
BROADWELL, R.	November 10, 1864	North Carolina	K	12th State Troop	833
BROMDER, J.W.	May 17, 1865	South Carolina	C	25th	2954
BROOK, T.D.	March 8, 1865	North Carolina	G	40th	2409
BROOKE, Benjamin H.	September 27, 1864	Virginia	I	26th	391
BROOKS, Andrew P.	June 15, 1865	South Carolina	G	1st Rifles	2879
BROOKS, Andrew T.	January 31, 1865	Virginia	A	19th Cavalry	1775
BROOKS, Archibald G.	August 10, 1864	Georgia	H	64th - Corporal	135
*BROOKS, D.H.	April 10, 1865	Georgia	G	11th	2542
*BROOKS, J.H.	April 10, 1865	Georgia	G	11th	2663

D. H and J. H. Brooks were both from the same Georgia regiment and *both share the same death date - April 10, 1865*. They were not brothers but possibly cousins. D. H. was David Hill Brooks. J. H. was John Hill Brooks. David enlisted into the 11th Regiment of Company G Infantry on May 7, 1862 at Tunnel Hill, Georgia. The 11th fought in most of the major battles with Robert E. Lee. At Gettysburg the 11th charged a Yankee regiment, on July 2 it chased another regiment through Devil's Den and advanced as far as Little Round Top. Though the 11th went on with Lee until the end of the War, David was wounded in the 2nd Battle of the Wilderness and left on the battlefield.

Captured by the Northern Army he became a prisoner of war on May 6, 1864. David was first went to Point Lookout Maryland, and later he was transferred to the Elmira Prison Camp, and arrived on August 14, 1864. David died at Elmira Prison on April 10, 1865, due to pneumonia one day after Lee surrendered to Grant. A mystery surrounds David's marker - why does he share the stone and number with S. H. Pedy? We may never know.

John's story is not known.

Name	Date of Death	State	Company	Regiment/Notes	Woodlawn
BROOKS, Thomas	December 24/64	North Carolina	D	33rd	1103
BROOKS, Thomas G.	October 16, 1864	Virginia	C	26th	554
BROOKS, William	February 24, 1865	North Carolina	F	5th Cavalry	2260
BROTHERTON, Elias M.	September 28, 1864	North Carolina	D	42nd	436
BROWN, A.	October 10, 1864	South Carolina	F	4th Cavalry	672
BROWN, A.	March 29, 1865	Virginia	G	25th	2493
BROWN, Bryant	April 16, 1865	North Carolina	D	1st Battalion of Artillery	2718
BROWN, Edward	March 23, 1865	South Carolina	E	11th	1607
BROWN, H.	March 11, 1865	South Carolina	H	22nd	1842
BROWN, H.H.	December 13, 1864	Alabama	F	59th – Sergeant	1133
BROWN, James A.	November 29, 1864	North Carolina	B	51st	999
BROWN, James H.C.	June 6, 1865	North Carolina	A	32nd – Corporal	2892
BROWN, James W.	December 20, 1864	Tennessee	B	1st	1075
BROWN, Jesse J.	April 29, 1865	South Carolina	L	1st – Sergeant	2731
BROWN, Joel	March 9, 1865	Florida	A	1st Reserve	1882
BROWN, John F.	February 9, 1865	North Carolina	F	52nd	1943
BROWN, Nathan	September 26, 1864	Georgia	H	7th – Sergeant	450
BROWN, P.A.	January 31, 1865	North Carolina	A	18th	1783
BROWN, Richard E.	October 1, 1864	South Carolina	G	21st	404
BROWN, T.J.	February 8, 1865	North Carolina	H	18th	1938
BROWN, T.S.	January 14, 1865	Georgia	B	7th	1472
BROWN, Thomas K.	March 13, 1865	Georgia	C	Phillips' Legion	2435
BROWN, W.B.	April 10, 1865	North Carolina	B	43rd	2603

Name	Date of Death	State	Company	Regiment/Notes	Woodlawn
BROWN, W.L.	September 18, 1864	North Carolina	B	56th	311
BROWN, William	October 16, 1864	North Carolina	F	18th	557
BROWN, William	February 28, 1865	North Carolina	G	13th	2127
BROWN, William A.	February 20, 1865	Tennessee	B	44th	2305
BROWNE, William	April 4, 1865		Confederate States Marine		2562
BROWNLEE, L.	May 16, 1865	South Carolina	G	11th	2961
BRYAN, Robert S.	November 28, 1864	South Carolina	A	27th	991
BRYANT, A.T.	December 16, 1864	North Carolina	F	18th	1275
BRYANT, Francis M.	March 1, 1865	North Carolina	D	18th	1777
BRYANT, Travers S.	July 15, 1864	North Carolina	I	51st	Shohola
BRYANT, William	January 28, 1865	South Carolina	D	18th	1652
BUCHANAN, Lorenzo D.	September 12, 1864	North Carolina	B	25th	183
BUCHANAN, Thomas T.	December 21, 1864	Virginia	I	50th	1328
BUCK, Samuel R.	December 10, 1864	North Carolina	E	41st	1153
BUCKNER, John J.	April 14, 1865	North Carolina	C	3rd	2708
BUCKNER, Thomas S.	April 25, 1865	North Carolina	I	45th	1414
BUFFKIN, Jordon W.	September 20, 1864	North Carolina	A	8th	324
BULLARD, J.J.	February 16, 1865	North Carolina	E	30th	2206
BULLARD, Jesse	February 15, 1865	North Carolina	E	36th	2182
BULLARD, William J.	February 27, 1865	North Carolina	K	40th, 3rd Artillery	2154
BULLOCK, John H.	October 6, 1864	Virginia	E	47th	645
BULMAN, J.L.	February 4, 1865	South Carolina	I	Holcombe Legion	1748
BUNBOUGH, Thomas	January 14, 1865	Tennessee	A	1st Artillery	1469

Name	Date of Death	State	Company	Regiment/Notes	Woodlawn
BUNDY, G.W.	March 5, 1865	South Carolina	F	21st	2377
BUNN, Sidney	April 6, 1865	North Carolina	H	32nd	2642
BUNNELL, Kenneth	October 7, 1864	Virginia	B	61st	650
BURCHAM, Jodel	March 2, 1865	Virginia	C	50th	2096
BURCHAM, S.W.	February 25, 1865	North Carolina	D	33rd	2275
BURDESHAW, John T.	March 23, 1865	Alabama	K	3rd	1518
BURDETT, Alfred W.	September 5, 1864	Alabama	B	13th	233
BURGAMY, William H.	February 12, 1865	Georgia	K	12th	2248
BURGESS, J.C.	July 10, 1865	South Carolina	I	25th	2844
BURGESS, J.W.	October 6, 1864	Virginia	I	5th Cavalry	590
BURGESS, Joseph	February 20, 1865	North Carolina	B	18th	2307
BURK, J.J.	April 11, 1865	South Carolina	G	27th	2675
*BURK, Isaac	June 25, 1865	Alabama	C	1st Battalion of Artillery	2822
BURKE, Joseph	January 22, 1865	Alabama	C	1st Battalion of Artillery	1601
BURKE, William	December 7, 1864	Alabama	B	3rd	1184
BURKETT, G.H.	March 11, 1865	Alabama	A	1st Battalion of Artillery	1845
*BURKETT John	February 25, 1865	North Carolina	D	1st Battalion of Artillery	2289
BURKETT, Joshua	January 4, 1865	Alabama	A	1st Battalion of Artillery	1248
BURLEYSON, William	March 9, 1865	North Carolina	C	42nd	1871
BURNELL, D.	February 27, 1865	North Carolina	H	51st	2160
BURNETT, John E.	December 7, 1864	South Carolina	C	22nd	1182
BURNETT, T.	November 7, 1864	North Carolina	F	31st	769
BURT, W.B.	August 30, 1864	South Carolina	H	17th	56

Name	Date of Death	State	Company	Regiment/Notes	Woodlawn
BURT, W.E.	November 12, 1864	North Carolina	I	12th	940
BURTON, John T.	November 5, 1864	North Carolina	B	8th	837
BURTON, Richard N.	March 20, 1865	North Carolina	G	40th	1573
BURTON, W.H.	September 7, 1864	Georgia	G	53rd	247
BUSH, Albert G.	February 2, 1865	Florida		Norwood's Militia - Corporal	1766
BUSH, James I	October 6, 1864	Virginia	H	5th	647
BUSHONG, John	January 29, 1865	Tennessee	E	63rd	1802
BUSKETT, J.W.	April 13, 1865	Virginia	E	50th	2680
BUTCHER, James E.	January 19, 1865	North Carolina	C	8th	1202
BUTLER, David	September 28, 1864	Georgia	E	51st	433
BUTLER, George A.	January 23, 1865	Florida		Rgt.	1610
BUTLER, John C.	January 4, 1865	North Carolina	C	30th	1247
BUTTS, J.A.	July 7, 1865	North Carolina	F	24th	2840
BUTTS, Matthew	November 11, 1864	North Carolina	K	1st	826
BUTTS, Thomas J.	January 14, 1865	Alabama	A	1st - Sergeant	1456
BYRD, John F.	December 2, 1864	Mississippi	D	17th - Sergeant	1007
BYRD, Robert	March 21, 1865	North Carolina	K	40th, 3rd Artillery	1534
CADE, Bonger	October 29, 1864	Virginia	B	15th	734
CAIN, Joshua	April 20, 1865	North Carolina	I	36th	1384
CAIN, M.	July 15, 1864	Virginia		Pegram's Battery - Artillery Shohola	
CALDWELL, David	February 27, 1865	Virginia	E	45th	2145
CALDWELL, William T.	December 29, 1864	AlabamaA		21st	1307
CALHOUN, Hugh C.	February 8, 1865	North Carolina	F	18th	1929

Foster's Pond still exists. This view is on the river levee looking west behind the Barracks No. 3 Memorial on Winsor Avenue.

Name	Date of Death	State	Company	Regiment/Notes	Woodlawn
CALHOUN, N.	September 14, 1864	South Carolina	F	Holcombe Legion	264
CALL, James H.	December 10, 1864	North Carolina	L	13th	1159
CALLAWAY, J.C.	April 8, 1865	North Carolina	I	52nd	2637
CALLEHAN, C.	July 17, 1864		C	10th Cavalry	Shohola
CALLIHAN, William J.	March 14, 1865	North Carolina	B	36th, 2nd Artillery	1661
CALVIN, John	December 17, 1864	Georgia	F	23rd	1280
CAMERON, R.F.	December 23, 1864	South Carolina	B	4th Cavalry	1092
CAMERON, William R.	March 12, 1865	Alabama	B	6th	1840
CAMPBELL, A.P.	March 22, 1865	North Carolina	H	30th	2441
CAMPBELL, Allen J.	January 3, 1865	Alabama	F	1st Artillery	1344
CAMPBELL, C.E.	February 19, 1865	North Carolina	B	36th	2316
CAMPBELL, Colin	March 2, 1865	North Carolina	G	40th	1999
CAMPBELL, D.D.	March 9, 1865	North Carolina	B	36th	1885
CAMPBELL, Eugene	January 10, 1865	Louisiana	F	1st Cavalry	1214
CAMPBELL, George	December 7, 1864	Tennessee	A	14th	1181
CAMPBELL, James	October 5, 1864	Georgia	B	44th	605
*CAMPBELL, John	July 15, 1865	Louisiana	I	3rd	2852
CAMPBELL, John N.	August 29, 1865	North Carolina	K	25th	2856
CAMPBELL, Leonard	March 28, 1865	North Carolina	B	18th	2485
CAMPBELL, Thomas	January 4, 1865	North Carolina	G	53rd	1250
CAMPBELL, W.A.	January 5, 1865	North Carolina	G	24th	1239
CANNON, James	April 10, 1865	North Carolina	G	40th	2667
CANNON, R.J.	March 9, 1865	North Carolina	K	25th	1872
CANTRELL, George W.	December 12, 1864	North Carolina	E	45th	1144

Name	Date of Death	State	Company	Regiment/Notes	Woodlawn
CANUP, Miles A.	November 2, 1864	North Carolina	K	8th	760
CAPE, Enoch A.	February 9, 1865	Georgia	A	24th	1955
CAPPS, Charles	June 30, 1865	North Carolina	E	1st	2831
CAPPS, John M.	January 1, 1865	North Carolina	E	1st	1331
CAPPS, W.C.	January 27, 1865	Alabama	L	3rd	1631
CARDWELL, James	September 5, 1864	Virginia	G	26th	235
CARDWELL, Joseph B.	October 20, 1864	Virginia	C	26th	878
CARLISLE, Dennis	September 29, 1864	North Carolina	D	51st	400
CARLTON, G.W.	February 6, 1865	North Carolina	G	18th	1905
CARLTON, J.B.	September 18, 1864	Georgia	F	16th	162
CARMAN, John	February 5, 1865	Alabama	E	12th	1908
CARMICHAEL, J.D.	March 30, 1865	South Carolina	L	21st	2592
CARMONCHE, Alcide	December 12, 1864	Louisiana	K	2nd Cavalry	1143
CARNES, Jonas	April 17, 1865	South Carolina	E	22nd	1356
CARNEY, Matthew V.	December 18, 1864	Missouri	F	1st Cavalry - Corporal	1279
CARPENTER, Jonas	October 18, 1864	North Carolina	D	1st Battalion	546
CARPENTER, Levi	March 1, 1865	North Carolina	I	37th - Corporal	2740
CARPENTER, Peter H	March 3, 1865	North Carolina	D	12th	2011
CARRAWAY, J.H.	November 24, 1864	South Carolina	K	23rd	914
CARROLL, Haywood	March 25, 1865	North Carolina	G	36th	2467
CARROLL, Henry W.	February 7, 1865	South Carolina	D	Hood's Battalion	1926
CARROLL, J.A.	May 16, 1865	North Carolina	G	36th	2962
CARROLL, James	March 9, 1865	North Carolina	K	40th	1874

Name	Date of Death	State	Company	Regiment/Notes	Woodlawn
CARROLL, Joel G.	March 10, 1865	North Carolina	G	36th	1879
CARROLL, L.W.	May 9, 1865	North Carolina	E	45th	2780
CARROLL, S.	March 23, 1865	Virginia	C	15th Cavalry	1520
CARROLL, W.J.	January 29, 1865	Virginia	I	15th Cavalry	1800
CARSON, Henry	March 18, 1865	North Carolina	H	23rd	1702
CARSON, James L.	February 21, 1865	South Carolina	B	1st Artillery	2238
CARSON, John M.	September 2, 1864	North Carolina	K	25th	81
CARTER, C.L.	August 12, 1864	North Carolina	F	5th	132
CARTER, James M.	October 11, 1864	Florida	K	5th	691
CARTER, Joseph R.P.	October 17, 1864	South Carolina	F	14th	543
CARTER, Richard	January 23, 1865	North Carolina	C	42nd	1599
CARTER, Samuel	January 26, 1865	Virginia	B	49th	1629
CARTER, Thomas P.	April 12, 1865	Virginia	F	50th	2681
CARY, J.W.	July 15, 1864	North Carolina	I	51st	Shohola
CASEY, Benjamin D.	February 28, 1865	North Carolina	G	40th	2139
CASEY, James A.	October 11, 1864	Virginia	B	48th	681
CASH, Green	December 18, 1864	North Carolina	A	24th	1064
CASHWELL, N.	March 6, 1865	North Carolina	H	13th	2379
CASON, Henry	December 19, 1864	Louisiana	B	3rd Cavalry	1065
CASTNER, J.P.	September 22, 1864	North Carolina	G	32nd	488
CATON, Elijah	February 26, 1865	North Carolina	D	53rd	2136
CAUTHORN, W.J.	February 26, 1865	North Carolina	I	15th	2279
CAVANAUGH, John	December 5, 1864	Virginia	E	51st - Sergeant	1030
CECIL, James L.	September 23, 1864	Virginia	F	29th	353

Name	Date of Death	State	Company	Regiment/Notes	Woodlawn Shohola
CENTER, C.O.	July 15, 1865	North Carolina	H	52nd	2253
CHAMBERS, James M.	February 22, 1865	Texas	E	7th	1053
CHAMBERS, Pleasant	December 10, 1864	Tennessee	I	44th	2347
CHAMBLISS, David	February 18, 1865	Alabama	E	1st Artillery	395
CHANCY, S.	September 28, 1864	South Carolina	I	27th	648
CHANDLER, George H.	October 6, 1864	North Carolina	H	24th	2655
CHAPMAN, A.A.	April 18, 1865	South Carolina	I	18th	2889
CHAPMAN, George W.	June 9, 1865	Alabama	B	1st Battalion of Artillery	858
CHAPMAN, Israel	October 24, 1864	Virginia	H	23rd	2119
CHAPMAN, P.H.	February 27, 1865	Virginia	D	42nd	425
CHAPMAN, R.	September 29, 1864	North Carolina	H	34th	1418
CHAPMAN, Thomas	April 26, 1865	North Carolina	F	8th	1161
CHAPMAN, W.S	December 8, 1864	Alabama	G	8th	207
CHARLES, Andrew	September 9, 1864	North Carolina	F	3rd	2444
CHATHAM, F.M	March 24, 1865	Georgia	C	7th Cavalry	1005
CHEEK, Nathaniel W.	December 1, 1864	North Carolina	B	1st	2858
CHERRY, Oliver	August 23, 1865	North Carolina	B	32nd - Sergeant	1134
CHEWING, J.S.M.	December 12, 1864	Virginia	D	26th	1826
CHRISTIAN, Merry	March 13, 1865	Georgia	H	8th	1037
CHURCH, Calvin	December 9, 1864	North Carolina	G	20th	1561
CHURCH, T.G	March 19, 1865	North Carolina	K	5th Artillery	1098
CHURCH, Thomas A.	December 23, 1864	Tennessee	A	1st Artillery	1566
CLAMPS, W.C.C.	March 20, 1865	North Carolina	E	1st Artillery	

Name	Date of Death	State	Company	Regiment/Notes	Woodlawn
CLANCY, Patrick	September 26, 1864	Louisiana	B	14th	446
CLANTON, D.C.	January 21, 1865	Georgia	H	7th Cavalry	1590
CLANTON, Francis	May 24, 1865	North Carolina	B	37th	2923
CLAPP, John	December 5, 1864	North Carolina	E	1st	1028
CLARK, Archibald	September 12, 1864	North Carolina	A	48th	195
CLARK, B.C.	March 8, 1865	North Carolina	I	31st	2372
CLARK, Benjamin	October 8, 1864	North Carolina	F	31st	658
CLARK, Henry C.	September 30, 1864	Virginia	B	20th	399
CLARK, John A.	April 19, 1865	North Carolina	K	8th	1376
CLARK, John E.	November 7, 1864	Virginia	K	26th	776
CLARK, W.	September 2, 1864	South Carolina	H	18th	78
CLARKE, Jasper N.	April 11, 1865	Georgia	E	Cobb's Legion	2693
CLAYTON, C.M.	October 6, 1864	North Carolina	D	8th	592
CLAYTON, F.R.	March 23, 1865	South Carolina	F	25th	2439
CLAYTON, J.W.	December 31, 1864	Alabama	I	7th Cavalry	1319
*CLAYTON, William T.	January 8, 1865	Florida		Goodwin's Company Militia	1498
CLEGG, Franklin	September 30, 1864	Virginia	H	26th	407
CLEGHORN, W.R.	May 19, 1865	Georgia	D	16th	2945
CLEM, James	October 10, 1864	Virginia	H	Imboden's Brigade - Signal Guard	675
*CLEMENTS, B.B.	March 8, 1865	Virginia	F	38th	2376
CLEPPER, Henry	November 11, 1864	Tennessee	A	14th	786
CLIFFORD, W.G.	May 12, 1865	North Carolina	G	5th	2797
CLIFTON, Riley	March 21, 1865	Virginia	K	48th	1536

Name	Date of Death	State	Company	Regiment/Notes	Woodlawn
CLIMBELL, John F.	March 16, 1865	Virginia	H	26th	1687
CLINE, Henry B.	May 28, 1865	North Carolina	E	4th Cavalry	2913
CLODFELTER, Henry	October 24, 1864	North Carolina	H	14th	713
CLOWER, Joseph G.	September 18, 1864	Georgia	E	64th	316
CLOWER, Noah L.	August 8, 1864	Alabama	G	61st	140
COATES, Cornelius R.	March 10, 1865	Virginia	B	26th	1862
COBB, C.H.	March 26, 1865	North Carolina	D	1st	2474
COBB, Stephen C.	April 9, 1865	Mississippi	K	12th	2616
*COCHRAN, A.W.	March 8, 1865	South Carolina	I	25th	2373
COCHRAN, Elijah P.	March 1, 1865	North Carolina	F	26th, 2nd Artillery-State Troop	2025
*COCHRAN, John	September 22, 1864	North Carolina	A	28th	478
COCHRAN, Robert J.	March 1, 1865	North Carolina	F	36th, 2nd Artillery-State Troop	2099
COFFEE, James	October 14, 1864	Virginia	I	50th	707
COGGIN, J.J.	July 5, 1865	North Carolina	H	36th	2837
COGGIN, James W.	January 17, 1865	North Carolina	H	32nd	1448
COGHILL, M.T.	September 2, 1864	North Carolina	D	8th	83
COKER, Asa	September 25, 1864	South Carolina	I	1st Artillery	375
COKER, J.S.	December 10, 1864	South Carolina	I	4th Cav.alry	1046
COKER, William B.	February 13, 1865	North Carolina	E	31st	2064
COLE, E.W.	September 19, 1864	South Carolina	I	Holcombe Legion	323
COLEMAN, Daniel	December 10, 1864	North Carolina	D	33rd	1033
COLEMAN, Issac M.	November 12, 1864	South Carolina	C	22nd	827
COLEMAN, J.D.	April 21, 1865	North Carolina	E	36th	1385

The Elmira Prison Camp officially opened on July 6, 1864. The first grave marker in Woodlawn National Cemetery bears the name William Garner. By the dates of death he would have actually been the ninth to die. The first eight were probably interred at the camp, then relocated to Woodlawn in July 1865 as their marker numbers are nearer the end.

Name	Date of Death	State	Company	Regiment/Notes	Woodlawn
COLEMAN, Jacob	December 24, 1864	Tennessee	F	63rd	1102
COLEMAN, Thomas	January 27, 1865	Georgia	G	3rd	1650
COLES, C.W.	September 28, 1864	Virginia	H	5th Cavalry - Corporal	445
COLEY, George	August 1, 1864	North Carolina	C	42nd	148
COLEY, I. A.	March 13, 1865	North Carolina	C	42nd	1817
COLEY, J.M.	April 7, 1865	North Carolina	I	8th	2647
COLEY, W.M.	March 5, 1865	North Carolina	D	5th	1974
*COLEY, Wesley	June 10, 1865	North Carolina	I	43rd	2888
COLLET, William	February 18, 1865	North Carolina	G	5th	2205
COLLINS, C.	August 7, 1864	North Carolina	I	53rd	11
COLLINS, Dallas	January 20, 1865	North Carolina	G	1st	1585
COLLINS, Jasper N.	September 24, 1864	North Carolina	I	53rd	384
*COLLINS, John R.	November 19, 1864	Virginia	F	5th	969
COLLINS, P.A.	April 11, 1865	South Carolina		4th	2698
COLLINS, R. H.	February 9, 1865	South Carolina	L	22nd	1948
COLLINS, S.I.	September 18, 1864	Georgia	I	14th	153
COLLINS, W.S.	March 22, 1865	Texas	E	Waller's Battalion-13th Cavalry	1521
COLTON, A. S.	March 31, 1865	North Carolina		Citizen of North Carolina	2532
COLVIN, John	January 19, 1865	Georgia	A	53rd	1203
CONE, John T.	June 4, 1865	North Carolina	C	1st	2896
CONLON, J.	September 22, 1864	South Carolina	K	27th	483
CONNELL, J.W.	March 3, 1865	Georgia	A	7th Cavalry	2015
CONNELLY, William C.	February 16, 1865	North Carolina	F	18th	2180

Name	Date of Death	State	Company	Regiment/Notes	Woodlawn
CONNOR, Nathan F.	September 21, 1864	Virginia	B	42nd	341
COOK, Henry C.	April 26, 1865	North Carolina	A	5th	1422
COOK, J.W.	January 4, 1865	Georgia	F	12th Battalion Light Artillery	1264
COOK, James C.	April 6, 1865	Tennessee	K	63rd	2719
COOK, Jesse	November 20, 1864	Georgia	H	64th	943
COOK, Joel R.	March 30, 1865	Virginia	L	4th	2527
COOK, W.D.	March 29, 1865	South Carolina	C	25th	2541
COOK, W. S.	August 30, 1864	North Carolina	I	7th – Sergeant	55
COOK, Young H.	August 20, 1864	North Carolina	I	25th	116
COONEY, Thomas	September 7, 1864	Alabama	I	61st	212
COOPER, C. H.	March 19, 1865	North Carolina	C	36th	1730
COOPER, Franklin	October 28, 1864	North Carolina	C	42nd	718
COOPER, H. B.	July 25, 1865	North Carolina	D	36th	2861
COOPER, J. R.	September 2, 1864	Georgia	I	7th Cavalry	84
COOPER, M.W.	February 22, 1865	Alabama	E	9th	2239
COOPER, Reuben H. W.	February 16, 1865	Georgia	C	9th	2186
COOPER, W.J.	November 5, 1864	South Carolina	G	7th	838
COPELAND, Barnabas	September 20, 1864	Tennessee	D	25th	497
CORBIN, Edward	May 23, 1865	South Carolina	D	11th	2926
CORBIN, Philip	March 24, 1865	Virginia		Citizen of Virginia	2460
*CORDER, D.A.	July 4, 1865	South Carolina	D	17th	2834
CORDER, John	October 1, 1864	North Carolina	G	28th	418
CORNELIUS, John W.	August 21, 1864	North Carolina	C	33rd	111

Name	Date of Death	State	Company	Regiment/Notes	Woodlawn
CORNELIUS, W. P.	March 22, 1865	Virginia	L	55th	1522
CORNIN, J.T.	April 8, 1865	North Carolina	G	45th	2635
COTTLER, L. D.	February 2, 1865	North Carolina	G	3rd	1761
COUCH, J.A.	February 12, 1865	South Carolina	E	18th	2056
COUCH, William D.	November 16, 1864	Georgia	C	Phillips Legion	956
COUGHTON, O.	February 24, 1865	North Carolina	H	10th	2271
COUNCIL, J.S.	November 17, 1864	North Carolina	B	37th	964
COUNTERS, C.	November 11, 1864	Virginia	E	50th	790
COURTNEY, W. C.	February 20, 1865	Virginia	I	10th	2329
COX, Daniel D.	March 7, 1865	Virginia	I	21st	2412
COX, Isaac B.	March 21, 1865	North Carolina	E	36th	1542
COX, John M.	September 2, 1864	North Carolina	H	28th	223
COX, Peter B.	April 16, 1865	North Carolina	B	31st	2715
COX, Thomas	January 27, 1865	Virginia	E	50th	1638
COZZENS, R. W.	March 19, 1865	North Carolina	D	13th Battalion Artillery	1565
COZZENS, T.F.	April 6, 1865	North Carolina	D	13th Battalion Artillery	2639
CRABTREE, Albert M.	February 21, 1865	Tennessee	B	23rd - Corporal	2319
CRABTREE, Gaston C.	November 1, 1864	North Carolina	C	22nd	748
CRAFT, Frederick	April 12, 1865	North Carolina	A	35th	2699
CRAFT, George W.	May 18, 1865	Alabama	C	6th	2949
CRAIG, Leslie C.	October 6, 1864	Georgia	C	9th	649
CRAVEN, Benjamin	February 18, 1865	North Carolina	H	3rd	2356
CRAVEN, Thomas	December 2, 1864	South Carolina	I	11th	1010

Name	Date of Death	State	Company	Regiment/Notes	Woodlawn
CRAWFORD, Joseph H.	September 7, 1864	Virginia	F	26th Battalion	216
CRAWFORD, Mathias	March 12, 1865	North Carolina	F	10th	1818
CRAWFORD, William E.D.	March 7, 1865	South Carolina	G	25th	2406
CREACH, D. L.	June 3, 1865	South Carolina	F	21st	2900
CREAMER, Adam	May 18, 1865	Virginia	F	25th	2950
CREEKMORE, Alex O.	September 26, 1864	Virginia	F	15th	452
*CREEKMORE, M.	September 22, 1864	Virginia	F	15th	490
CREESE, R.J.	April 28, 1865	North Carolina	K	8th – Sergeant	2732
CREPPS, J.	February 27, 1865	North Carolina	E	5th	2128
CRESS, John A.	September 16, 1864	North Carolina	G	7th	298
CRESSEL, M.	February 20, 1865	Tennessee	F	63rd	2350
CREWS, M. L.	October 9, 1864	Georgia	G	7th Cavalry	655
CRISWELL, Jacob D.	August 27, 1864	North Carolina	C	57th	30
CROCKER, W. D.	March 25, 1865	Confederate States Navy "Bombshell" Seaman			2455
CRONE, James	September 5, 1864	Virginia	A	26th Battalion	236
CROSBY, J.N.	September 26, 1864	Mississippi	B	48th	455
CROUCH, John	October 26, 1864	North Carolina	I	2nd	853
CROUCH, T. B.	May 8, 1865	Georgia	D	8th	2775
CROWDER, Lucanus	October 4, 1864	North Carolina	H	31st	636
CROWNOVER, Joseph	December 30, 1864	Alabama	C	1st Battalion of Artillery	1311
CRUSE, Asa	September 21, 1864	Virginia	G	42nd	339
CRUTCHFIELD, R. F.	January 30, 1865	Georgia	E	7th Cavalry	1793
CULBERTH, D.M.	February 21, 1865	North Carolina	B	36th	2265

Name	Date of Death	State	Company	Regiment/Notes	Woodlawn
CULLIN, James	October 23, 1864	Alabama	C	61st	860
CUMBEE, B.	March 18, 1865	North Carolina	D	36th Artillery	1557
CUMBEE, Solomon	April 12, 1865	North Carolina	D	36th Artillery	2684
CUNNINGHAM, Adam	September 18, 1864	Virginia	E	4th	154
CUNNINGHAM, W.J.	March 26, 1865	Kentucky	E	2nd	2476
CUPP, Jesse	September 18, 1864	Virginia	F	7th Cavalry	522
CURRIE, N.R.	May 14, 1865	South Carolina	F	21st	2802
CURRIN, Wyatt	February 13, 1865	North Carolina	I	23rd	2195
CURRY, George	November 7, 1864	Georgia	F	48th	778
CURRY, Sam	November 14, 1864	Florida	G	9th	808
CURRY, William H.	February 23, 1865	Virginia	F	50th	2256
CURTIS, Hiram L.	November 21, 1864	Louisiana	G	3rd	931
CURTIS, Samuel	February 23, 1865	North Carolina	K	38th	2246
CUTCHIN, W.T.	March 11, 1865	North Carolina	F	36th	1837
CYPHERS, Aaron	September 25, 1864	Virginia	E	50th	358
DAILEY, Benjarrin F.	March 4, 1865	North Carolina	G	40th	1984
DALE, James C.	March 27, 1865	North Carolina	D	36th	2528
DALTON, Nicholas	January 13, 1865	Virginia	H	42nd	1473
DAME II, John M.	September 22, 1864	Georgia	B	12th	482
DANCY, J.M.	January 3, 1865	North Carolina	G	18th	1507
DANIEL, Elisha	January 25, 1865	Georgia	I	12th	1615
DANIEL, Henry	April 17, 1865	North Carolina	F	10th, 1st Artillery-State Troop	1363

Name	Date of Death	State	Company	Regiment/Notes	Woodlawn
DANIEL, James H.	August 12, 1864	North Carolina	G	8th	129
DANIEL, M.E.	March 28, 1865	North Carolina	G	36th	1670
DANIEL, W.W.	September 5, 1864	North Carolina	I	12th	238
DANIEL, William	December 25, 1864	Florida	A	1st	1112
DANIELS, James W.	October 17, 1864	Florida	K	8th	549
DANIELS, L.	April 14, 1865	South Carolina	B	15th Cavalry	2704
DANNELLY, James W.	February 14, 1865	Georgia	G	12th	2029
DANTZLER, B.M.	February 20, 1865	South Carolina	F	25th – Sergeant	2588
DANTZLER, David W.	April 1, 1865	South Carolina	G	25th	2588
DARDEN, Daniel	April 2, 1865	North Carolina	C	3rd	2571
DARING, I. S.	May 20, 1865	South Carolina	E	11th	2940
DARNELL, M.V.	March 28, 1865	Virginia	C	48th – Sergeant	2518
DAVID, John W.	February 15, 1865	Georgia	C	Cobb's Legion	2184
DAVIDSON, F. L.	December 15, 1864	Alabama	A	Cavalry	1061
DAVIDSON, J.T.	May 10, 1865	North Carolina	D	1st Battalion	2786
DAVIDSON, James	September 11, 1864	Virginia	I	Hood's Brigade	295
DAVIDSON, Oscar	February 12, 1864	Texas	G	34th Cavalry	1145
DAVIDSON, W.	September 25, 1864	North Carolina	E	18th	456
DAVIS, Alexander	February 18, 1865	North Carolina	H	36th, 2nd Artillery-State Troop	2346
DAVIS, Alpheus L.	November 26, 1864	North Carolina	G	2nd	978
DAVIS, Amos L.	March 28, 1865	North Carolina	I	36th, 2nd Artillery-State Troop	2486
DAVIS, Benjamin	January 24, 1865	Virginia	B	6th Cavalry	1622

The Confederate Prisoners' Monument at Woodlawn National Cemetery was erected in 1937 by the United Daughters of the Confederacy.

Name	Date of Death	State	Company	Regiment/Notes	Woodlawn
DAVIS, Burwell	February 9, 1865	North Carolina	C	66th	1941
DAVIS, D. D.	February 7, 1865	North Carolina	K	43rd	1923
DAVIS, Drury T.	March 27, 1865	North Carolina	F	1st	2501
DAVIS, Ervin A.	February 1, 1865	North Carolina	D	57th	1757
DAVIS, Frank H.	November 7, 1864	Tennessee	H	63rd	774
DAVIS, H.	May 26, 1865	North Carolina	I	25th	2920
DAVIS, Henry E.	October 31, 1864	Virginia	H	15th Cavalry	735
DAVIS, J. P.	November 30, 1864	Tennessee	H	63rd - Corporal	996
DAVIS, John D.	July 15, 1864	North Carolina	I	51st	Shohola
DAVIS, L. A.	April 10, 1865	Louisiana	G	15th	2669
DAVIS, Meridith C.	December 20, 1864	North Carolina	A	1st	1076
DAVIS, Nathaniel S.	October 13, 1864	Georgia	I	18th	702
DAVIS, Robert	February 12, 1865	North Carolina	A	8th	2055
DAVIS, S.J.	December 14, 1864	Virginia	A	24th - Corporal	1127
DAVIS, Thomas J.	October 8, 1864	Georgia	H	9th	659
DAVIS, William D.	August 16, 1864	North Carolina	B	45th	123
DAVIS, William H.	April 27, 1865	North Carolina	C	36th	1428
DAVIS, Willis D.M.	June 4, 1865	Alabama	C	1st	2898
DAWKINS, J. T.	August 23, 1864	South Carolina	D	17th	35
DAWSON, J. B.	Arpil 24, 1865	North Carolina	I	18th	1407
DAWSON, W. W.	October 10, 1864	Virginia	F	50th	689
DAWSON, William S.	March 17, 1865	North Carolina	H	45th	1691

Name	Date of Death	State	Company	Regiment/Notes	Woodlawn
DAY, Benjamin S.	December 6, 1864	Louisiana	A	1st – Nelligan's Infantry	1024
DAY, Eli	April 21, 1865	North Carolina	A	4th	1390
DAY, F.M.	August 28, 1864	North Carolina	A	24th	47
DEAL, David L.	April 10, 1865	North Carolina	G	37th–Sergeant–NC Troops	2673
DEAL, M.M.	April 20, 1865	North Carolina	A	12th	1380
DEALL, Peter H.	February 15, 1865	Virginia	C	22nd	2168
DEAN, Dempsey	January 13, 1865	North Carolina	E	7th	1485
*DEAN, John	January 27, 1865	Alabama	A	1st Battalion of Artillery	1642
DEANS, Daniel O.	August 23, 1864			Citizen	36
DECK, G.W.	September 16, 1864	Tennessee	F	63rd	171
DEERMAN, H.	February 27, 1865	Virginia	I	50th	2111
DEES, J.A.	February 27, 1865	North Carolina	B	26th	2140
DELOACH, Nelson	March 4, 1865	South Carolina	I	25th	1980
DENNIS, J.H.	March 29, 1865	Virginia	A	6th Cavalry	2519
DENTON, S.J.	February 3, 1865	Tennessee	F	63rd	1745
DERMING, Francis	December 15, 1864	Mississippi	A	10th Cavalry	1117
DERRING, John	December 13, 1864	Mississippi	K	42nd	1135
DESHOZO, James M.	March 18, 1865	Alabama	C	16th	1559
DEVER, N.H.	July 15, 1864	North Carolina	I	51st	Shohola
DEVINNEY, Robert	December 4, 1864	North Carolina	G	12th	885
DIAL, Jacob	March 19, 1865	South Carolina	F	21st	1583
DIAMOND, G.W.	December 10, 1864	North Carolina	F	45th	1042

Name	Date of Death	State	Company	Regiment/Notes	Woodlawn
DICKENS, J.	March 18, 1865	North Carolina	F	36th - Sergeant	1692
DICKINS, W. B.	March 23, 1865	North Carolina	K	1st	1516
DICKINSON, Samuel H.	January 3, 1865	Virginia	E	25th	1336
DICKINSON, William M.	December 18, 1864	South Carolina	D	18th	1066
DICKSON, K.	February 4, 1865	Georgia	B	7th Cavalry	2259
DIDDY, James R.	April 5, 1865	North Carolina	E	53rd	2545
DIGGS, W. Riley	November 26, 1864	North Carolina	B	31st	980
DILLAHAY, John T.	December 10, 1864	North Carolina	A	24th	1155
DILLON, J.H.	December 11, 1864	North Carolina	L	21st	1051
DILLON, Robert	September 7, 1864	Alabama	G	6th	222
DILLON, S.	August 15, 1864	Virginia	B	58th	125
DINAN, Cornelius	August 14, 1864	South Carolina	H	27th	22
DINGUS, Jasper W.	January 14, 1865	Virginia	A	5th - Sergeant	1465
DIXON, James	September 25, 1864	Georgia	E	7th Cavalry	369
DIXON, James D.	March 28, 1865	North Carolina	A	1st Cavalry	2489
DIXON, William	March 17, 1865	North Carolina	I	18th	1707
DOBBS, William U.	November 8, 1864	Alabama	A	21st	785
DOBSON, Charles	January 3, 1865	South Carolina	E	11th	1348
DODD, Thomas A.	March 12, 1865	Georgia	A	24th	1838
*DODDRIDGE, W.	April 17, 1865	North Carolina	H	32nd	1358
DOLITTLE, B.	October 30, 1864	North Carolina	K	1st	746
DONALD, Robert A.	October 27, 1864	Virginia	H	4th	720

Name	Date of Death	State	Company	Regiment/Notes	Woodlawn
DONNEGAN, Ashley	February 28, 1865	North Carolina	F	3rd	2125
DOOLEY, Jackson H.	September 9, 1864	Virginia	AB	5th	203
DORKINS, W. C.	September 4, 1864	South Carolina	G	17th	229
DORMAN, John	September 9, 1864	North Carolina	E	8th	205
DOUGH, John C.	November 22, 1864	North Carolina	B	8th	928
DOUGH, Thomas T.	April 2, 1865	North Carolina	B	8th	2572
DOUGHERTY, Charles L.	January 31, 1865	Georgia	D	3rd Battalion Sharpshooters	1780
DOUGHTIE, Aipheus P.	February 24, 1865	North Carolina	C	3rd Artillery	2261
DOUGHTRY, William M.	January 18, 1865	Virginia	I	61st - Sergeant	1432
DOUGLASS, D. E.	September 25, 1864	Georgia	E	7th Cavalry	376
DOUGLASS, Henry	April 2, 1865	South Carolina	D	21st Artillery	1699
DOUGLASS, James W	October 13, 1864	Tennessee	I	14th	574
DOUGLASS, John F.	December 11, 1864	Texas	G	2nd Cavalry	1149
DOUGLASS, W. W.	February 17, 1865	South Carolina	B	1st Rifles	1915
DOVER, Muston H.	April 25, 1865	Alabama	C	1st Battalion of Artillery	1415
DOWDY, R. C.	September 24, 1864	North Carolina	D	61st	465
DOWDY, William A.	October 10, 1864	Virginia	A	58th	688
DOWDY, William E.	March 12, 1865	South Carolina	G	31st	1830
DOWDY, William H.	October 19, 1864	Virginia	G	3rd Cavalry	535
DOWNES, J.	October 19, 1864	Alabama	F	1st Battalion of Artillery	877
DOWNING, Valentine	April 5, 1865	North Carolina	F	3rd	2552
DOXY, John V.	November 13, 1864	North Carolina	B	8th	818

Name	Date of Death	State	Company	Regiment/Notes	Woodlawn
DOYLE, Jacob	September 18, 1864	Virginia	B	31st	512
DOYLE, John	March 3, 1865	Virginia	G	31st	2012
DOYLE, Joseph H.	September 28, 1864	Virginia	A	24th	393
DOZIER, J. F.	March 8, 1865	North Carolina	E	36th	1877
DRAKE, H.	February 15, 1865	North Carolina	H	6th	2194
DREW, James F.	February 27, 1865		Confederate States Marine		2121
DRUMMOND, W.H.	September 19, 1864	Georgia	F	18th	499
*DRY, J.A.	March 14, 1865	North Carolina	H	8th	1995
DUDLEY, Sampson	May 26, 1865	North Carolina	A	36th	2918
DUKE, G. L.	November 26, 1864	Louisiana		Citizen of Louisiana	977
DUKE, H.M.	April 30, 1865	Tennessee	A	23rd	2734
DUKE, Martin V.	June 23, 1865	Alabama	C	3rd	2816
DUKE, William P.	January 28, 1865	Alabama	F	1st Artillery	1657
DUNCAN, George W.	January 14, 1865	South Carolina	F	Holcombe Legion-Corporal	1461
DUNCAN, J.J.	March 30, 1865	North Carolina	F	36th	2600
DUNCAN, James	September 29, 1864	Virginia	C	46th	432
DUNCAN, John	November 14, 1864	Georgia	E	24th - Sergeant	813
DUNCAN, Noah	January 13, 1865	Virginia	C	50th	1487
DUNCAN, Robert	December 12, 1864	North Carolina	G	45th	1056
DUNN, F. H.	April 9, 1865	North Carolina	D	40th	2618
DUNN, George	December 1, 1864	North Carolina	K	30th	1008

Name	Date of Death	State	Company	Regiment/Notes	Woodlawn
DUNN, Thomas J.	September 11, 1864	Virginia	C	Youngs Battery-1st Regiment	196
DYER, James	January 16, 1865	Virginia	E	6th Cavalry	1452
EADS, George W.	December 21, 1864	Virginia	C	29th	1084
EARLEY, Moses	February 12, 1865	North Carolina		3rd Battalion Light Artillery	2047
EARLEY, T.J.	September 20, 1864	North Carolina	G	32nd	517
EARLS, Daniel	April 1, 1865	North Carolina	K	10th	2594
EASTERLING, H.J.	May 26, 1865	South Carolina	F	21st	2917
EASTRIDGE, John W.	February 3, 1865	South Carolina	E	27th	1890
EBBERHART, J. B.	October 3, 1864	Georgia	D	7th Cavalry	614
ECCLES, James C.	March 13, 1865	North Carolina	F	13th	1819
ECHOLS, W. E.	March 23, 1865	Virginia	G	6th Cavalry - Corporal	1512
EDENY, A.	October 3, 1864	North Carolina	B	32nd	611
EDGER, Robert D.	March 20, 1865	North Carolina	I	36th	1718
EDINGTON, James P.	January 15, 1865	Virginia	E	42nd	1463
EDWARDS, Calvin	November 14, 1864	North Carolina	E	24th	811
EDWARDS, Edward F.	March 11, 1865	North Carolina	H	32nd, 2nd Artillery	1849
EDWARDS, 3. H.	March 28, 1865	North Carolina	F	33rd	2483
EDWARDS, John	February 10, 1865	Florida	A	5th Cavalry	1957
EDWARDS, John H.	December 29, 1864	Virginia	B	26th	1318
EDWARDS, Oliver P.	September 10, 1864	North Carolina	K	16th	254
EDWARDS, Samuel A.	September 25, 1864	North Carolina	G	28th	373

Looking east toward Davis Street from the Confederate Prisoners' Monument.

Name	Date of Death	State	Company	Regiment/Notes	Woodlawn
EDWARDS, Thomas	January 7, 1865	North Carolina	C	37th	1233
EDWARDS, Walter	October 14, 1864	North Carolina	D	30th	708
EGERTON, W. B.	August 22, 1864	Virginia	B	Malone's Battalion-Sergeant	38
EGGLESTON, James L.	September 16, 1864	Virginia	F	42nd	169
ELARBEE, Nathaniel	October 30, 1864	Georgia	K	7th Cavalry	739
ELDER, William C.	November 24, 1864	North Carolina	K	7th	917
ELFER, E.	December 22, 1864	Louisiana	A	Miles Legion-Cavalry	1090
ELLER, David	March 10, 1865	Virginia	D	42nd	1855
ELLER, Jacob F.	February 10, 1865	Georgia	D	24th	1953
ELLIOTT, James W.	September 8, 1864	Georgia	F	3rd	214
ELLIS, Charles S.	March 28, 1865	North Carolina	B	10th, 1st Artillery	2502
ELLIS, Duville	October 14, 1864	North Carolina	F	9th	674
ELLIS, E. S.	May 17, 1865	South Carolina	C	25th	2953
ELLIS, H. C.	December 6, 1864	Virginia	H	26th	1187
ELLIS, Samuel	January 24, 1865	South Carolina	B	23rd	1619
ELLIS, W. W.	March 6, 1865	South Carolina	B	21st	1961
ELLIS, Wiley J.	January 30, 1865	North Carolina	G	7th Cavalry	1315
*ELLISON, James	January 8, 1865	South Carolina	E	Hampton's Legion	1503
ELMORE, John	February 28, 1865	Virginia	K	46th	2149
ELMORE, Mark	December 12, 1864	Florida		Florida Miltia	1137
ELWOOD, Elmice	April 17, 1865	Virginia	K	40th	1355
ENDY, John F.	March 28, 1865	North Carolina	F	5th	1857

Name	Date of Death	State	Company	Regiment/Notes	Woodlawn
EPPS, E.	August 16, 1864	North Carolina	D	14th	26
ERWIN, A. S.	October 29, 1864	South Carolina	K	Holcombe Legion	731
ESKEW, R. B.	March 19, 1865	Virginia	A	36th - Corporal	1572
ESKRIDGE, John H.	November 9, 1864	Georgia	D	20th Battalion Cavalry-Sergeant	835
ESTES, Lindsey A.	December 23, 1864	Virginia	D	34th	1094
ESTES, William F.	December 9, 1864	Virginia	G	26th	1166
ETHERNAGE, Moses A.	March 13, 1865	North Carolina	H	31st	1825
EURE, F. H.	January 9, 1865	North Carolina	E	33rd	1228
EURE, Elisha	February 2, 1865	North Carolina	E	7th	1768
EURE, W. W.	March 29, 1865	North Carolina	F	26th	2525
EVANS, C. H.	July 21, 1865	South Carolina	I	25th	2866
*EVANS, J. A.	December 28, 1864	North Carolina	I	18th	1295
EVANS, R. N.	June 2, 1865	South Carolina	F	25th - Corporal	2903
EVENS, Daniel	February 9, 1865	North Carolina	I	26th	1942
EVERETT, Jordan	January 13, 1865	North Carolina	G	8th	1455
EVERS, Dennis	March 29, 1865	North Carolina	K	40th, 3rd Artillery State Troop	2512
EVERS, Ephriam	March 14, 1865	North Carolina	K	40th	1675
EVERS, Phillip	April 14, 1865	North Carolina	B	18th - Sergeant	2710
EVERS, William H.	March 27, 1865	North Carolina	K	40th, 3rd Artillery State Troop	2478
EXUM, Benjamin	March 10, 1865	North Carolina	F	10th	2361
FAIRBURN, J. A.,	February 21, 1865	Virginia	C	2nd	2299
FAIRCLOTH, Daniel	December 29, 1864	North Carolina	E	8th	1316

Name	Date of Death	State	Company	Regiment/Notes	Woodlawn
FAIRCLOTH, Reason	November 14, 1864	North Carolina	E	8th	804
FAIRCLOTH, T.	March 17, 1865	North Carolina	E	36th	1703
FAIRCLOTH, Thomas H.	March 14, 1865	North Carolina	C	36th, 2nd Artillery	2430
FALKNER, Benjamin	December 6, 1864	North Carolina	D	14th	1032
FALLS, William W.	March 8, 1865	Virginia	C	10th	2370
FANE, Abraham	September 7, 1864	Virginia	K	50th	218
FANK, John C.	January 27, 1865	Tennessee	A	1st Artillery	1636
FARRAR, Samuel	September 14, 1864	North Carolina	G	45th	272
FARRIS, William H. H.	January 26, 1865	Virginia	D	48th	1632
FARRON, Joel	November 11, 1864	Georgia	H	24th	823
FAULK, T. D.	October 3, 1864	North Carolina	C	18th	629
FAULK, William R.	January 28, 1865	North Carolina	C	18th	1658
*FAULKNER, W. L.	September 17, 1864	South Carolina	I	17th	309
FAUNT, C.M.	March 20, 1865	South Carolina	C	4th	1574
FAWCITT, Robert J.	April 3, 1865	North Carolina	E	1st	2634
FELKEL, Wesley R.	June 2, 1865	Florida	K	5th	2901
FELLOWS, Henry	February 21, 1865	North Carolina	A	1st	2323
FELT, Nathaniel G.	September 9, 1864	North Carolina	C	12th	198
FELTON, J.L.	April 22, 1865	Texas	H	35th Cavalry - Corporal	1395
FENNELL, James R.	October 9, 1864	Florida	F	5th	660
FENNELL, William M.	September 6, 1864	South Carolina	G	22nd	221
FEREBEE, Granby	February 12, 1865	Virginia	E	61st	2078
FERGUSON, Thomas B.	December 18, 1864	Virginia	C	50th	1277

Name	Date of Death	State	Company	Regiment/Notes	Woodlawn
FIBBS, R.J.	February 3, 1865	North Carolina	A	1st	1751
FIELDS, A.M.	February 13, 1865	North Carolina	C	3rd	2041
FIELDS, J.B.	September 16, 1864	Georgia	G	35th	165
FIELDS, John	April 24, 1865	Florida	B	5th	1405
FIELDS, John	November 14, 1864	North Carolina	E	8th	953
FIELDS, R.J.	March 5, 1865	Georgia	E	Phillip's Legion	1969
FIELDS, Tobias	March 4, 1865	North Carolina	G	40th	2002
FIKE, C.E.	March 16, 1865	Alabama	K	8th	1678
FINLEY, C.N.	July 3, 1865	Virginia	F	6th Cavalry - Corporal	2833
FISHER, M.T.	March 2, 1865	North Carolina	C	36th	2747
FISHER, Solomon C.	October 17, 1864	North Carolina	A	34th	547
FISHER, William D.	December 18, 1864	Virginia	I	16th Cavalry	1281
FITTINGTON, John	March 11, 1865			General's Escort	2660
*FLANAGAN, Barney	April 6, 1865	Alabama	A	1st Battalion of Artillery	1467
FLEENOR, Harvey G.	January 13, 1865	Virginia	I	48th	45
FLEENOR, William H.	August 29, 1864	Virginia	H	48th	1946
FLEMING, Isaac	February 9, 1865	North Carolina	A	54th	31
FLEMING, John W.	August 21, 1864	Virginia	F	26th	1423
FLEMING, S.W.	April 26, 1865	South Carolina	I	25th	1637
FLETCHER, William A.	January 27, 1865	North Carolina	D	24th	182
FLINT, Ezekiel	September 12, 1864	Virginia	E	26th	2712
FLIPPIN, H.	April 11, 1865	Virginia	C	44th	2498
FLOWERS, Andrew	March 29, 1865	South Carolina	B	21st	479

Corporal Michel Fortlouis
Pointe Coupée Artillery

submitted by Diane Janowski

Allen Smith and I are double historians – in our hometown of Elmira, New York and in our adopted hometown of New Roads, Louisiana. In New Roads (Pointe Coupée Parish) we are involved in several history projects including the Pointe Coupée at the Millennium photography project.

We often discuss the differences and similarities between the North and the South. During a March 2006 visit to Pointe Coupée Parish, we spent an evening with Pointe Coupée historian Brian Costello and began a conversation about the Civil War. A question came up – Elmira had the infamous Elmira Prison Camp between 1864 and 1865 – did Costello know of any Pointe Coupée soldiers who were sent to Elmira? He believed there was one – named Fortlouis. Interest piqued in us – who was this soldier and what circumstances brought him from New Roads to Elmira. Before leaving Louisiana, we stopped along a sugar cane field on Gremillion Road and collected a bag of Pointe Coupée dirt. I had a purpose.

Back home in Elmira, I began research. Between internet history sites and emails to Mr. Costello, I pieced the information together and found Michel Fortlouis.

Number 995 in the death list of 2,963 Confederate prisoners of war, Corporal Michel Fortlouis died at the Elmira Prison Camp in Elmira, New York. Fortlouis and his two brothers, Leopold and Theophile, enlisted in the Pointe Coupée (Louisiana) Artillery Company B in June 1861. The Pointe Coupée Artillery Company B fought at the siege of Vicksburg, and with its losses was consolidated into Company A, which joined the Army of Tennessee and was active in the Atlanta Campaign. Michel Fortlouis, however, went missing at about the same time as the beginning of the Atlanta Campaign in April/May 1864. Union troops captured Michel Fortlouis in Clinton, Louisiana on August 20, 1864. He was received at Ship Island, Mississippi on October 5, 1864, subsequently received in New York City on November 16, 1864, arrived at the Elmira Prison Camp on November 19, 1864, and died in Barracks No. 3 on November 29, 1864 of pneumonia – just ten days after arriving in Elmira. His marker is erroneously marked "L. Forthewis." Michel Fortlouis was 27-years old. Both his brothers survived the war.

On Memorial Day 2006, we visited Fortlouis' grave in Woodlawn Cemetery, and in a quiet personal ceremony, we gave him the dirt from home, and affixed his marker with his correct information. It has since become a Memorial Day tradition for us to visit Michel.

Woodlawn National Cemetery is a beautiful well-kept place and it is always most beautiful on Memorial Day. The groundspeople do an immaculate job.

Our own Memorial Day ceremony, 2006.

Elmira Prison Camp

Name	Date of Death	State	Company	Regiment/Notes	Woodlawn
FLOWERS, Henry	September 22, 1864	Virginia	F	4th	1660
FLOWERS, J.A.	March 15, 1865	South Carolina	F	4th	2273
FLOYD, John W.,	February 25, 1865	Alabama	E	1st Battalion of Artillery	723
FLOYD, Thomas	October 27, 1864	Virginia	E	44th	20
FLYNN, John	August 15, 1864	South Carolina	C	27th	1502
FLYTHE, Henry T.	January 7, 1865	North Carolina	D	32nd	1502
FLYTHE, J.F.A.	November 27, 1864	Virginia	A	25th – Sergeant	902
FOGLES, W.G.	March 16, 1865	South Carolina	F	25th	1679
FOLDS, George W.	December 14, 1864	Georgia	E	64th	1121
FOLEY, Coleman	November 18, 1864	Virginia	G	25th	967
FOLKS, James A.	March 14, 1865	North Carolina	A	36th	1672
FORD, David R.	April 19, 1865	Georgia	E	64th	1375
FORD, John J.	February 26, 1865	Virginia	F	26th	2162
FORD, Joshua	January 1, 1865	Virginia	A	48th – Corporal	1139
FOREMAN, J.K.	August 27, 1864	Georgia	G	7th Cavalry - Sergeant	98
FOREMAN, John W.	February 12, 1865	Virginia	G	61st	2053
FOREMAN, Joshua B.	December 6, 1864	North Carolina	A	17th	1025
FORT, John H.	May 10, 1865	North Carolina	F	24th	2791
FORT, W.H.	December 18, 1864	North Carolina	H	14th	1276
*FORTHEWIS, Lewis	November 29, 1864	Louisiana	A	Pointe Coupée Artillery	995
FORTNER, B.F.	August 15, 1864	Virginia	H	5th	21
FOSTER, Burt H.	October 2, 1864	North Carolina	B	24th	632

Name	Date of Death	State	Company	Regiment/Notes	Woodlawn
FOSTER, D.	March 4, 1865	South Carolina	H	22nd	2420
FOSTER, E.M.	September 4, 1864	Virginia	H	26th	226
FOSTER, James B.	December 7, 1864	Georgia	K	21st	1183
*FOSTER, Thomas	June 12, 1865	North Carolina	E	42nd	2884
FOUNTAIN, William	February 21, 1865	Georgia	G	7th Cavalry	2234
FOWLER, Hosea	February 3, 1865	South Carolina	K	27th	1750
*FOWLER, J.S.	January 28, 1865	Texas		Collin's Cavalry	1654
FOWLER, Newton F.	August 31, 1864	South Carolina	F	18th	93
FOWLER, William B.	January 3, 1865	Alabama	A	21st	1337
FOX, Isaiah	April 3, 1865	North Carolina	G	40th, 3rd Artillery-State Troop	2561
FOX, Wesley	January 30, 1865	North Carolina	G	37th	1794
FRANCIS, Presley	September 27, 1864	North Carolina	A	2nd	392
FRANKLIN, Ennis	March 6, 1865	Alabama	A	1st Artillery	2387
FRANKLIN, William	November 2, 1864	Virginia	D	59th	755
FRANKLIN, William	March 29, 1865	Virginia	D	5th Cavalry	2479
FREDRICK, Alfred E.	December 4, 1864	North Carolina	B	3rd	886
FREDRICK, Elisha	January 22, 1865	North Carolina	D	3rd	1592
FREEMAN, G.W.	September 20, 1864	North Carolina	H	1st	329
FREEMAN, George	February 25, 1865	South Carolina	D	25th	2270
FREEMAN, William	February 9, 1865	North Carolina	G	40th, 3rd Artillery-State Troop	1939
FRIAR, William	January 25, 1865	Alabama	G	9th	1618
FRICK, Daniel	January 29, 1865	North Carolina	I	5th	1805

Confederate markers in Woodlawn National Cemetery.

Name	Date of Death	State	Company	Regiment/Notes	Woodlawn
FRIDDLE, Lewis	August 29, 1864	North Carolina	H	1st	51
FRY, Allen H.	September 23, 1864	Virginia	A	42nd - Sergeant	475
FUGET, R.	April 1, 1865	Virginia	I	50th	2593
FULCHER, Spencer S.	April 1, 1865	Virginia	H	58th - Corporal	2597
FULKS, William	March 20, 1865	North Carolina	G	21st	1550
FULLER, Byam	July 15, 1864	Georgia	H	24th	Shohola
FULLER, Robert	October 19, 1864	South Carolina	H	7th	533
FULTON, William T.	August 18, 1864	Georgia	K	4th	122
FUNDERBURG, William M.	November 1, 1864	Alabama	D	12th	747
FUNDERBURK, L. N.	May 26, 1865	South Carolina	E	22nd	2921
FURGERSON, Allen	August 22, 1864	North Carolina	E	3rd	33
FURGERSON, August	February 22, 1865	North Carolina	C	35th	2302
FURGUSON, D.	March 10, 1865	North Carolina	C	3rd	1868
FURGUSON, George S.	January 5, 1865	South Carolina	A	17th - Sergeant	1257
FURR, Lawson A.	December 6, 1864	North Carolina	K	28th	1191
FURR, Martin	February 23, 1865	North Carolina	C	3rd	2242
FUTCH, J.I.	August 11, 1864	Georgia	H	7th Cavalry	136
FUTCH, Stephen	February 23, 1865	Florida	D	9th	2268
FUTRAL, L.	August 25, 1864	North Carolina	E	56th	44
FUTRELL, Noah	December 10, 1864	North Carolina	D	32nd	1047
GABRIEL, Andrew J.	January 4, 1865	Florida	F	6th	1269
GAINES, D.F.	May 8, 1865	North Carolina	F	10th	2278

Name	Date of Death	State	Company	Regiment/Notes	Woodlawn
GAINES, W.J.	March 4, 1865	North Carolina	K	10th	2001
GAITHER, John R.	September 16, 1864	Virginia	B	10th	301
GALASPY, W.	May 8, 1865	Virginia	F	30th	2776
GALAWAY, P.	March 7, 1865	South Carolina	H	21st	2397
GALBREATH, Malcolm	September 2, 1864	North Carolina	D	51st	70
GALLAWAY, Charles W.	September 12, 1864	Virginia	C	26th	190
GALLAWAY, John	February 13, 1865	North Carolina	E	52nd	2042
GALLIHAN, George	April 14, 1865	Virginia	B	Pegram's Battery	2705
GALLOWAY, L. C.	April 25, 1865	South Carolina	B	21st	1417
*GAMBLE, F. E.	April 7, 1865	South Carolina	I	25th	2645
GAMMA, H. A.,	April 27, 1865	Virginia	G	23rd	2722
GANAE, D.	February 13, 1865	Louisiana	B	Edward's Battalion	2062
GANEY, G. W.,	September 4, 1864	South Carolina	E	21st	74
GARDNER, A.M.	August 3, 1864	Virginia	G	26th	3
GARDNER, Robert	March 2, 1865	North Carolina	E	36th	2018
GARDNER, W.B.	March 5, 1865	North Carolina	F	10th	2375
GARDNER, William C.	January 1, 1865	North Carolina	E	55th	1329
GARGANOUS, James R.	September 17, 1864	North Carolina	H	1st	161
GARNER, A. G.,	April 27, 1865	Georgia	E	12th - Light Artillery	2723
GARNER, William	July 27, 1864	Virginia	G	27th	1
GARNETT, Richard	March 7, 1865	Virginia	G	26th	2362
GARRETT, W. H.,	March 30, 1865	North Carolina	B	20th	2531

Name	Date of Death	State	Company	Regiment/Notes	Woodlawn
GARRIES, B. C.	April 9, 1865	North Carolina	G	8th	2620
GASQUETT, W. H.	January 19, 1865	Louisiana	I	2nd Cavalry	1586
GATES, Joseph J.	September 29, 1864	Virginia	D	44th	435
GATTON, W. F.,	July 15, 1864	Virginia	B	35th Cavalry	Shohola
GEORGE, Thomas A.,	November 25, 1864	Virginia	A	40th	916
GERNER, A. C.	March 23, 1865	North Carolina	E	1st	1513
GIBBS, William	February 28, 1865	Virginia	A	30th Battery	2113
GIBBS, William F.	September 12, 1864	North Carolina	B	22nd State Troop	188
GIBSON, Ebenezer B.	March 10, 1865	North Carolina	E	40th, 3rd Artillery-State Troop	1883
GIBSON, Henry W.	November 5, 1864	North Carolina	A	32nd	764
GIBSON, J.M.	March 19, 1865	North Carolina	H	35th	1732
GIBSON, William J.,	November 26, 1864	Alabama	F	3rd	979
GILLESPIE, W.J.	October 4, 1864	Virginia	E	50th - Corporal	635
GILMORE, Richard	January 13, 1865	Virginia	F	2nd	1466
GIPSON, N.	March 14, 1865	North Carolina	A	45th	1662
GIRARDEAU, C.G.	February 22, 1865	Georgia	B	20th	2306
GLADDEN, Silas	February 15, 1865	South Carolina	D	7th	2176
GLASQUE, S.O.	March 28, 1865	South Carolina	A	21st	2503
GLASS, David D.	September 21, 1864	Virginia	G	59th - Sergeant	335
GLASS, J. C.	November 14, 1864	Tennessee	D	63rd	801
GLAUSIER, William T.	March 24, 1865	Georgia	D	64th	2454
GLEATON, Joseph T. S.	March 28, 1865	Georgia	D	64th	2490

Name	Date of Death	State	Company	Regiment/Notes	Woodlawn
GLENN, Michael	January 31, 1865	South Carolina	C	27th	1772
GLIMPSE, J.L.	March 29, 1865	North Carolina	C	6th Cavalry	2516
GLOVER, Eli S.	February 16, 1865	Alabama	F	1st Battalion of Artillery	2215
GOFF, George A	August 7, 1864	Virginia	E	19th Cavalry	12
GOLDON, W.B.	November 8, 1864	Alabama	F	1st Battalion of Artillery	783
GOODE, A.W.	October 15, 1864	Virginia	B	26th	553
GOODE, James T.	September 20, 1864	Virginia	B	26th	509
GOODE, Thomas	January 9, 1865	Virginia	C	26th	1218
GOODMAN, Christopher C.	October 2, 1864	Georgia	G	44th – Sergeant	633
GOODMAN, Henry	February 21, 1865	North Carolina	G	26th	2237
GOODSON, George W.	December 11, 1864	Louisiana	H	8th	1048
GOODSON, J.C	August 16, 1864	Georgia	K	7th Cavalry	27
GOODSON, William	September 26, 1864	Georgia	E	21st	449
GORDON, James M.	October 25, 1864	North Carolina	I	2nd Cavalry - Corporal	849
GOSHLING, G.W.	May 15, 1865	South Carolina	H	22nd	2806
GOWEN, A.	September 21, 1864	Virginia	H	5th	484
GOWER, H.S.	May 14, 1865	North Carolina	D	36th	2800
GRACE, Caleb S.	February 17, 1865	Virginia	B	48th	2217
*GRAHAM, Daniel	July 24, 1864	North Carolina	I	51st	2848
GRAHAM, David E.	April 12, 1865	Virginia	BH	25th	2685
GRAHAM, James	February 01, 1865	South Carolina	D	25th	1887
GRANGER, Joseph D.	January 11, 1865	Louisiana	K	10th	1212

Name	Date of Death	State	Company	Regiment/Notes	Woodlawn
GRANT, Barnabas	January 31, 1865	South Carolina	E	4th Cavalry	1778
GRANT, Solomon E.	March 6, 1865	North Carolina	K	10th, 1st Artillery	2411
GRANTHAM, Josiah L.	March 23, 1865	North Carolina	E	40th, 3rd Artillery	1514
GRANTHAM, R.W.	March 5, 1865	South Carolina	H	2nd	2398
GRAVES, J.B.	December 2, 1864	North Carolina	G	5th	892
GRAY, O.B	November 2, 1864	Georgia	K	7th Cavalry	752
GRAY, P.W.	February 13, 1865	South Carolina	F	21st	2063
GREEN, A.J.	May 21, 1865	North Carolina	B	22nd	2936
GREEN, E.	May 4, 1865	South Carolina	C	23rd	2760
GREEN, H.W.	August 26, 1864	North Carolina	C	23rd	101
GREEN, Henry	July 15, 1864	Virginia	A	9th	Shohola
GREEN, J.L.	October 4, 1864	North Carolina	H	30th	600
GREEN, Wyatt B.	March 28, 1865	Alabama	A	1st Battalion of Artillery	2014
GREEN, Z.P.	November 15, 1864	Alabama	A	1st Battalion of Artillery	810
GREGORY, John	December 9, 1864	South Carolina	A	18th	1164
GREGORY, William	September 17, 1864	North Carolina	E	51	318
GRENOBLES, R.B.	September 8, 1864	South Carolina	I	20th	215
GREY, J.H.	September 22, 1864	Virginia		Citizen of Virginia	489
GRICE, N.E.	September 19, 1864	Georgia	K	7th Cavalry	321
GRIER, G.W.	March 22, 1865	North Carolina	A	36th	1517
GRIER, W.S.	March 12, 1865	South Carolina	A	21st	1852
GRIFFIN, A.B.	May 6, 1865	South Carolina	F	25th	2765

Name	Date of Death	State	Company	Regiment/Notes	Woodlawn
GRIFFIN, E.	February 5, 1865	North Carolina	E	45th	1909
GRIFFIN, H.J.F.	May 16, 1865	South Carolina	F	25th	2963
GRIFFIN, Jackson I.	January 21, 1865	Georgia	H	12th	1588
GRIFFIN, James L.	September 18, 1864	Virginia	K	19th Cavalry	515
GRIFFIN, John	January 22, 1865	North Carolina	E	48th	1602
GRIFFIN, John H.	January 8, 1865	Georgia	H	45th	1224
GRIFFITH, B.	November 6, 1864	North Carolina	C	32nd	773
GRIFFITH, William A. C.	October 12, 1864	Alabama	E	61st	566
GRIMSTEAD, D. N.	October 19, 1864	Virginia	C	13th Cavalry	540
GRIMSTEAD, W. F.	December 10, 1864	Virginia	G	49th	1152
GRISSARD, John E.	September 25, 1864	Virginia		Conscript	1186
GROSS, John G.	December 7, 1864	South Carolina	B	15th	1294
GROVES, Jacob R.	December 27, 1864	Virginia	B	10th	1458
GRUBBS, R.S.	January 14, 1865	Virginia	E	44th	1458
GRUMON, E.	February 26, 1865	Louisiana		Citizen of Louisiana	2297
GUERRANT, William L.	September 12, 1864	Virginia	C	44th – Sergeant	189
GUILLEN, G.W.	September 23, 1864	Virginia	D	50th	473
GUNTER, Thomas	December 4, 1864	Florida	K	9th	889
GUTHRIE, Benjamin	November 6, 1864	Virginia	H	14th	763
GUYER, William	January 3, 1865	Georgia	E	7th Cavalry	1268
GWIN, Robert H.	December 26, 1864	Virginia	B	26th	1286
HADAWAY, J.P.M.	November 11, 1864	Georgia	F	24th	795

Name	Date of Death	State	Company	Regiment/Notes	Woodlawn
HADDOCK, John B.	September 25, 1864	North Carolina	C	13th	374
HADEN, J.M.	October 11, 1864	Virginia	G	5th Cavalry	576
HAGLER, John M.	December 2, 1864	North Carolina	B	18th	900
HAGLER, William C.	September 3, 1864	North Carolina	B	18th	66
*HAILEY, H. A.	March 12, 1865	South Carolina	I	25th	1821
HAINES, John	February 5, 1865	Tennessee	B	1st Artillery	1898
HALE, Aaron K.	September 4, 1864	Florida	D	5th - Corporal	230
HALE, Henry I.	September 20, 1864	Florida	A	5th	495
HALE, Leander	September 2, 1864	Virginia	F	4th	80
*HAILEY, H.	June 17, 1865	Virginia	H	5th	2878
HALL, Alexander	April 2, 1865	North Carolina	D	11th	2581
HALL, C. H.	December 30, 1864	Virginia	D	42nd	1313
HALL, Charles	February 5, 1865	Alabama	E	1st Battalion of Artillery	1892
HALL, D. L.	March 19, 1865	North Carolina	C	36th	1564
HALL, Daniel	April 24, 1865	South Carolina	G	21st	2281
HALL, G.S.	March 1, 1865	North Carolina	H	36th	2109
HALL, J.H.	August 29, 1865	South Carolina	K	21st	2857
HALL, James	October 13, 1864	Virginia	D	42nd	698
HALL, James B.	February 15, 1865	Georgia	G	49th	2201
HALL, James E.	February 10, 1865	Alabama	E	1st Battalion of Artillery	2091
HALL, Jesse	February 10, 1865	North Carolina	I	36th	2093

Name	Date of Death	State	Company	Regiment/Notes	Woodlawn
HALL, Jesse	August 11, 1864	North Carolina	H	34th	137
HALL, John	September 26, 1864	Virginia	B	50th	453
HALL, Lewis	March 7, 1865	North Carolina	C	30th	1960
HALL, Thomas	February 14, 1865	North Carolina	B	6th	2204
HALL, W. A.	March 9, 1865	Alabama	B	22nd	1873
HALL, W. C.	March 4, 1865	Virginia	D	45th - Sergeant	1996
HALL, William	March 16, 1865	Virginia	B	50th	1685
HALL, William C.	October 27, 1864	North Carolina	K	2nd Cavalry	726
HAM, William B.	July 15, 1864	North Carolina	E	8th - Sergeant	Shohola
HAMER, James C.	March 2, 1865	South Carolina	F	21st	2022
HAMILTON, Henry C.	October 6, 1864	Georgia	K	12th	646
HAMILTON, William W.	November 16, 1864	Georgia	K	12th - Corporal	962
HAMMOND, J.E.	November 23, 1864	North Carolina	E	44th	924
HAMMONDS, T. B.	December 12, 1864	Virginia	E	50th	1140
HAMPTON, R. F.	October 9, 1864	Virginia	A	3rd Cavalry	697
HANCHEY, J.W.	March 20, 1865	North Carolina	B	3rd	2142
HANCOCK, William P.	November 14, 1864	Virginia	E	50th	792
HANEY, William E.	February 19, 1865	Virginia	C	4th	2358
HARCUM, Phillip E.	August 3, 1864	Virginia	L	55th	2
HARDIN, Jacob	September 18, 1864	Georgia	B	64th	519
HARDISON, J.J.	July 15, 1864	North Carolina	I	51st	Shohola
HARDY, J.W.	February 25, 1865	Georgia	H	26th	1531

The camp's original flagpole now stands next to the Barracks No. 3 monument on Winsor Avenue next to the Elmira Water Board pump station.

Name	Date of Death	State	Company	Regiment/Notes	Woodlawn
HARDY, Thomas	March 21, 1865	Georgia	K	27th	1227
HARGET, John M.	January 8, 1865	North Carolina	A	48th	1299
HARLEY, John W. C.	December 27, 1864	Virginia	I	48th	1299
HARMON, Abel	September 12, 1864	North Carolina	C	28th	186
HARMON, Erastus F.	January 13, 1865	Virginia	I	16th Cavalry	1482
HARN, W.I.	November 5, 1864	Georgia	H	7th Cavalry	775
HARNICK, E.	November 18, 1864	North Carolina	E	34th	950
HARP, W. H.	January 18, 1865	North Carolina	G	20th	1430
HARRALSON, Barley	January 19, 1865	North Carolina	A	13th	1208
HARRELL, Abner	December 30, 1864	North Carolina	K	1st	1320
HARRELL, Asa T.	January 18, 1865	North Carolina	B	23rd	1490
HARRELL, R.E.	June 12, 1865	Georgia	A	16th	2883
HARRIS, Darrell P.	June 21, 1865	Alabama	F	3rd	2811
HARRIS, Edward	April 2, 1865	North Carolina	G	36th	2585
HARRIS, Elisha	December 15, 1864	Virginia	G	42nd	2172
HARRIS, Henry	September 13, 1864	Virginia	A	42nd	263
HARRIS, J.W.	June 24, 1865	North Carolina	F	1st	2820
HARRIS, James A.	September 21, 1864	Virginia	A	8th Cavalry	485
HARRIS, Joseph	October 10, 1864	Mississippi	A	15th	684
HARRIS, Joseph H.	November 6, 1864	Virginia	A	41st	770
HARRIS, Wilson W.	January 29, 1865	North Carolina	A	32nd – Sergeant	1795
HARRISON, Benjamin L.	April 17, 1865	Georgia	C	49th	1353

Name	Date of Death	State	Company	Regiment/Notes	Woodlawn
HARRISON, J.J.	January 17, 1865	Alabama	A	1st Battalion of Artillery	1447
HARRISON, Levich B.	December 6, 1864	North Carolina	H	1st - Sergeant	1026
HARROLD, Elias	September 11, 1864	Virginia	K	25th	261
HART, T.J.	November 1, 1864	Virginia	C	59th - Corporal	750
HARTELL, Bartlett	March 29, 1865	North Carolina	E	37th	2488
HARTMAN, J.W.	September 14, 1864	North Carolina	H	53rd	268
HARTNESS, J.R.	March 20, 1865	South Carolina	C	17th	1570
HARTZOCK, George H.	January 18, 1865	Virginia	D	22nd Cavalry	1435
HARVESTON, George	April 15, 1865	Georgia	F	12th Artillery	2709
HARVILLE, A.J.	January 19, 1865	Alabama	C	12th	1198
HASELDEN, H.G.	January 6, 1865	South Carolina	F	4th Cavalry	1243
HASKINS, W.M.	March 21, 1865	North Carolina	D	40th	1529
HASSETT, John	October 20, 1864	Tennessee	I	17th	532
HASSLER, C. H.	February 6, 1865	South Carolina	F	21st	1919
HASTE, Calvin A.	February 14, 1865	North Carolina	C	3rd Artillery	2060
HATCH, J. S.	July 15, 1864	Georgia	H	53rd	Shohola
HATCHER, J.J.	September 15, 1864	Virginia	H	5th	158
HATCHER, John P.	March 6, 1865	Alabama	H	11th	1959
HATCHER, S. M.	August 6, 1864	Tennessee	E	63rd	10
HATCHER, S. O.	September 24, 1864	Virginia	F	42nd	458
HATCHER, W.M.	June 29, 1865	South Carolina	D	21st	2826
HATFIELD, James W.	April 29, 1865	South Carolina	E	7th	2730

Name	Date of Death	State	Company	Regiment/Notes	Woodlawn
HATFIELD, William	November 17, 1864	Georgia	B	Cobb's Legion	812
HATHCOCK, Calvin	November 3, 1864	North Carolina	C	42nd	759
HATLEY, John M.	November 21, 1864	North Carolina	H	8th	938
HATLEY, W. W.	May 16, 1865	North Carolina	H	8th	2958
HATTON, William L.	December 24, 1864	Louisiana		5th Battalion - Sergeant	1101
HAWKINS, Maj. B.	February 13, 1865	North Carolina	F	36th	2046
HAWKINS, William L.	March 16, 1865	Louisiana	L	1st	1684
HAWSE, L. A.	November 11, 1864	Alabama	F	1st Battalion of Artillery	831
HAYDEN, George W.	November 11, 1864	Virginia	I	48th	796
HAYES, C. F.	March 23, 1865	South Carolina	D	25th	1515
HAYNE, Joseph B.	December 10, 1864	North Carolina	K	43rd	1168
HAYNES, Henry H.	December 13, 1864	Georgia	A	45th	1141
HAYNES, Isaac B.	October 13, 1864	Virginia	I	25th - Sergeant	569
HAYNES, R. P.	July 15, 1864	Virginia	H	26th - Sergeant	Shohola
HAZELWOOD, John W.	October 7, 1864	Virginia	D	22nd	588
HEAD, William E.	February 17, 1865	Alabama	A	1st Artillery	2231
HEADY, Charles	May 27, 1865	North Carolina	D	36th	2914
HEALD, S. L.	February 11, 1865	Georgia	A	20th Battalion Cavalry	2079
HEARD, J.C.W.	March 10, 1865	Georgia	E	19th	1860
HEARON, Edward L.	December 11, 1864	Alabama	I	5th	1041
HECKLE, A.J.	February 9, 1865	South Carolina	F	25th	1951
HEDGEPATH, John S.	February 10, 1865	North Carolina	F	36th	1945

Name	Date of Death	State	Company	Regiment/Notes	Woodlawn
HEFNER, Samuel N.	February 17, 1865	North Carolina	E	6th Cavalry	2214
HELBRITH, G. W.	September 3, 1864	Tennessee	F	63rd	224
HELFER, Pleasant E.	December 2, 1864	North Carolina	K	42nd	893
HELTON, Hollis	September 14, 1864	North Carolina	E	48th	284
HENDERSON, A.	December 26, 1864	South Carolina	H	22nd	1292
HENDRICK, John E.	February 28, 1865	Virginia	G	3rd Cavalry	2118
*HENDRICK, Levi	January 14, 1865	North Carolina	E	32nd	1470
HENDRICK, N. B.	March 28, 1865	South Carolina	C	22nd	2487
HENDRICKS, George	October 28, 1864	Virginia		Citizen of Virginia	724
HENDRICKS, Lemuel S.	January 19, 1865	Florida	E	2nd	1481
HENDRICKS, T. M	November 14, 1864	South Carolina	K	27th	817
HENNING, Lorenzo D.	January 24, 1865	Virginia	F	22nd	1624
HENSON, J. B.	April 7, 1865	North Carolina	E	36th	2636
HERRIN, J.	June 4, 1865	Alabama	H	15th	2895
HERRING, Benjamin	May 22, 1865	North Carolina	G	40th	1386
HERRING, James	April 21, 1865	North Carolina	G	40th	622
HERRING, Oliver	October 3, 1864	North Carolina	F	51st	1910
HESTER, David D.	February 6, 1865	North Carolina	K	40th	1910
HESTER, Jasper	February 28, 1865	North Carolina	K	40th	2133
HESTER, Stephen	September 20, 1864	North Carolina	E	28th	350
HESTER, William J.	March 9, 1865	North Carolina	K	3rd Artillery	2589
HEWITT, J.R.	March 15, 1865	North Carolina	B	36th	1680

Name	Date of Death	State	Company	Regiment/Notes	Woodlawn
HEYGOOD, Jesse M.	September 19, 1864	South Carolina	F	7th	500
HIBBLE, Michael C.	January 27, 1865	Virginia	C	24th Cavalry	1647
HICKMAN, Eli	January 27, 1865	North Carolina	G	26th	1640
HICKMAN, H.	May 4, 1865	Virginia	A	6th Infantry	2803
HICKMAN, Robert	December 6, 1864	North Carolina	C	30th	1022
HICKMAN, William	February 28, 1865	North Carolina	E	36th	2117
HICKS, G. F.	March 31, 1865	North Carolina	G	40th	2599
HICKS, J.D.	September 12, 1864	Georgia		20th Cavalry	179
HICKS, John	September 2, 1864	Virginia	A	22nd	63
HICKS, John C	October 19, 1864	Georgia	A	24th	530
HICKS, Payton	September 30, 1864	North Carolina	I	1st Cavalry	405
HICKS, Thornton	February 13, 1865	North Carolina	F	21st	2048
HICKSON, W. L.	October 6, 1864	South Carolina	H	26th	584
HIGDON, J. T.	January 11, 1865	Alabama	A	1st Battalion of Artillery	1483
HIGGS, William	November 16, 1864	Virginia	A	59th	957
HILDEBRAND, D.	February 20, 1865	North Carolina	B	54th	2333
HILDRETH, Thomas	March 2, 1865	North Carolina	G	40th, 3rd Artillery	2007
HILL, Eli	May 22, 1865	South Carolina	B	21st	2744
HILL, James	March 25, 1865	Georgia	B	Cobb's Legion	2464
HILL, James J.	October 14, 1864	South Carolina	I	18th	704
HILL, John	October 19, 1864	Virginia	G	42nd - Sergeant	538
HILL, John W.	December 15, 1864	Virginia	H	50th-Wise Yankee Catchers	1060

Name	Date of Death	State	Company	Regiment/Notes	Woodlawn
HILL, M. R.	January 12, 1865	Georgia	F	60th - Sergeant	1195
HILL, Thomas W.	April 18, 1865	North Carolina	H	26th	1491
HILL, W.	December 8, 1864	Georgia	A	7th Cavalry	1179
HILL, William H.	November 13, 1864	Georgia	G	60th	814
HINES, G.W.	April 13, 1865	Texas	I	34th Cavalry	2702
HINES, Henry	March 26, 1865	North Carolina	A	40th	2465
HINES, John H.	January 26, 1865	North Carolina	E	16th - Sergeant	1633
HINES, Neill H.	March 18, 1865	North Carolina	D	18th	1725
HINES, Thomas	September 27, 1864	North Carolina	K	66th	462
HINKLE, William	November 22, 1864	Virginia	H	19th Cavalry	937
HINSON, E. A.	March 13, 1865	North Carolina	B	36th	2431
HINSON, Jacob	March 7, 1865	North Carolina	E	36th	2401
HINSON, John	May 18, 1865	South Carolina	E	21st	2947
HINSON, Rowan	September 22, 1864	South Carolina	C	42nd - Sergeant	481
HINTON, G. W.	September 17, 1864	North Carolina	C	24th	212
HIOTT, L. P.	October 24, 1864	South Carolina	I	11th	850
HIX, James P.	November 8, 1864	Tennessee	A	17th	791
HOBBS, George A.	March 31, 1865	North Carolina	K	10th Artillery - Corporal	1546
HOCKADAY, B.	March 5, 1865	South Carolina	A		1966
HODGE, George W.	April 6, 1865	Alabama	C	6th	2659
HODGE, J. B.	April 10, 1865	South Carolina	I	25th	2606
HODGE, William H.	March 7, 1865	South Carolina	K	21st	2392

A serene view of Confederate markers at Woodlawn National Cemetery looking west.

Name	Date of Death	State	Company	Regiment/Notes	Woodlawn
HODGERSON, Lewis	January 17, 1865	Alabama	A	1st Battallion of Artillery	1437
HODGES, S. B.	February 11, 1865	South Carolina	I	25th	2175
HODGES, T. J.	November 22, 1864	Georgia	H	7th Cavalry	965
HODGES, T. R.	October 3, 1864	Virginia	F	59th	615
HODGES, William	September 11, 1864	Virginia	C	46th	260
HODGINS, W. H.	March 9, 1865	Virginia	D	26th	1875
HODGINS, William B.	September 20, 1864	South Carolina	C	1st	325
HOFFMAN, A.	April 6, 1865	South Carolina	F	25th	2641
HOFFMAN, Waldemar	December 29, 1864	Texas	Os	Gidding's Battalion	1304
HOLCOMB, Sherwood	March 20, 1865	Georgia	B	64th	1568
HOLCOMB, William M.	March 17, 1865	Georgia	C	24th	1711
HOLDEN, N. B.	March 1, 1865	Texas	C	7th	2107
HOLDEN, N. E.	February 28, 1865	North Carolina	G	36th	2130
HOLDEN, S. H.	July 21, 1865	Georgia	E	5th	2865
HOLDEN, William F.	October 4, 1864	North Carolina	F	2nd	609
HOLLAND, Matthew	April 7, 1865	North Carolina	C	36th	2657
HOLLIDAY, J. D.	September 16, 1864	North Carolina	H	1st	166
HOLLIMAN, S. B.	September 27, 1864	Georgia	C	20th Cavalry	382
HOLLIMAN, William N.	August 27, 1864	Georgia	E	12th	106
HOLLINGSWORTH, Harrison	January 23, 1865	Virginia	I	42nd	1608
HOLLINSWORTH, D. S.	February 23, 1865	North Carolina	K	32nd	2266
HOLLIS, James	February 16, 1865		CAPT	Citizen	2178

Name	Date of Death	State	Company	Regiment/Notes	Woodlawn
HOLMAN, J. B.	January 3, 1865	North Carolina	H	5th Cavalry	1265
HOLMES, Harrison	October 8, 1864	Virginia		Citizen of Virginia	661
HOLMES, Matthew	January 18, 1865	Virginia	I	14th Cavalry	1434
HOLSONBACH, Robert	August 9, 1864	North Carolina	E	35th	139
HOLSTEIN, J.A.	March 7, 1865	South Carolina	G	25th	2381
HOLT, D. C.	February 14, 1865	Louisiana	E	12th Artillery	2164
HOLT, M.N.	July 17, 1865	Alabama	C	12th	2870
HONEYCUTT, J.T.	September 24, 1864	South Carolina	C	1st - Corporal	471
HOOD, Bold Robin	October 26, 1864	North Carolina	E	24th - Sergeant	854
HOOD, James	March 28, 1865	South Carolina	G	21st	2509
HOOKS, Daniel	September 19, 1864	Georgia	B	51st - Lee Guards	511
HOOKS, L. P.	March 8, 1865	South Carolina	C	25th	2374
HOOTER, John W.	December 17, 1864	Mississippi	A	Wood's Cavalry	1283
HOPKINS, George W.	April 24, 1865	Virginia	D	48th	1408
HOPKINS, Luke	February 20, 1865	North Carolina	H	1st	2314
HOPKINS, W.	October 5, 1864	North Carolina	I	1st	601
HORN, Daniel W.	March 26, 1865	North Carolina	C	36th	2470
HORN, Pleasant	September 25, 1864	North Carolina	H	30th	378
HORNE, W.J.	March 7, 1865	North Carolina	C	36th	2399
HORTTREE, Richard	February 19, 1865	Louisiana	B	Clark's Battalion - Sergeant	2324
HOUGH, Daniel	July 13, 1865	North Carolina	F	48th	2876
HOUSE, James M.	February 26, 1865	Georgia	C	24th	2137

Name	Date of Death	State	Company	Regiment/Notes	Woodlawn
HOUSE, John W.	September 26, 1864	North Carolina	H	8th	457
HOWARD, G.W.	January 19, 1865	North Carolina	D	18th	1199
HOWARD, H. H.	February 13, 1865	North Carolina	F	13th – Sergeant	2032
HOWARD, J.W.	October 24, 1864	North Carolina	K	22nd	847
HOWARD, John J.	November 24, 1864	Alabama	F	1st Battalion of Artillery	926
HOWARD, John L.	March 16, 1865	South Carolina	I	17th	1705
HOWARD, Joseph	September 28, 1864	South Carolina	A	21st	394
HOWARD, Joseph M.	February 18, 1865	North Carolina	G	30th	2351
HOWARD, William	May 1, 1865	North Carolina	D	1st Artillery	2736
HOWARD, William	October 12, 1864	North Carolina	E	61st	696
HOWE, David R. T.	May 1, 1865	Alabama	I	13th – Corporal	2742
*HOWE, J.T.	September 24, 1864	South Carolina	G	18th	459
*HOWE, Nathaniel L.	November 28, 1864	South Carolina	B	22nd	930
HOWELL, L. D.	May 22, 1865	North Carolina	F	10th	2933
HOWELL, Thomas	April 18, 1865	Georgia	H	64th	1360
HOWITT, D.W.	March 26, 1865	North Carolina	G	36th	2468
HOYLE, William H.	February 18, 1865	Florida	M	2nd	2223
HUCKS, Eldred	March 3, 1865	North Carolina	K	1st	1990
HUDSON, Benjamin G.	September 16, 1864	Virginia	B	15th Cavalry	310
HUDSON, E.G.	February 26, 1865	South Carolina	C	1st – Sergeant	2286
*HUDSON, J. B.	February 19, 1865	Georgia	B	25th–Bartow Avengers	2331
HUDSON, W. A.	September 9, 1864	South Carolina	B	2nd	202

Name	Date of Death	State	Company	Regiment/Notes	Woodlawn
HUDSON, William	December 10, 1864	North Carolina	C	5th	1045
HUFF, George P.	August 16, 1864	Tennessee	I	62nd	124
HUFFORD, John	April 10, 1865	Virginia	I	50th	2664
HUGGINS, W.J.	September 25, 1864	South Carolina	I	21st	385
HUGHES, Daniel	March 17, 1865	North Carolina	L	22nd	1713
HUGHES, Melcajah	October 19, 1864	Virginia	G	6th Cavalry	539
HUGHES, Miles	December 25, 1864	North Carolina	G	32nd	1110
HUITT, A. M.	February 28, 1865	North Carolina	E	32nd	2143
HULL, S.	March 18, 1865	South Carolina	E	11th	1723
HUMPHREY, J.W.	April 4, 1865	North Carolina	H	3rd Cavalry	2661
HUMPHREY, Martin	Septembr 26, 1864	North Carolina	B	24th	380
HUMPHREYS, E.	November 10, 1864	North Carolina	C	3rd	779
HUMPHRIES, W. L.	October 1, 1864	South Carolina	E	27th	404
HUNGERFELER, J.J.	February 13, 1865	South Carolina	G	27th	2068
HUNT, W.H.	February 23, 1865	Georgia	A	61st	2262
HUNT, William A.	March 14, 1865	Virginia	G	26th	2422
HUNTER, Stephen	September 14, 1864	Tennessee	D	25th	278
HURLEY, Daniel	December 15, 1864	Louisiana	G	Miles Legion	1119
HURT, Kindred	December 8, 1864	South Carolina	C	1st	1189
*HURT, Thomas W.	July 22, 1864	Virginia	I	20th	2849
HUSLESS, G. W.	March 9, 1865	South Carolina	F	21st	2515
HUTCHINSON, A. J.	February 28, 1865	North Carolina	A	30th	2124

The Confederate graves are marked with pointed stones. These stones replaced old wooden markers in 1907.

Name	Date of Death	State	Company	Regiment/Notes	Woodlawn
HYPES, John H.	August 22, 1864	Virginia	C	26th Battalion	32
IKNER, Ward	November 18, 1864	North Carolina	G	51st	970
INGRAM, David B.	January 28, 1865	Georgia	D	12th	1496
INMAN, William P.	February 6, 1865	Virginia	A	4th	1913
IRBY, P. S.	September 27, 1864	Lousiana	A	9th	390
IRWIN, Freeman	February 7, 1865	Florida	Jones Company	Florida Home Guards–1st Reserve	1930
IRWIN, W.J.	August 28, 1864	South Carolina	B	Hampton's Legion	49
ISRAEL, John	September 6, 1864	North Carolina	E	51st	242
ISRAEL, Joseph	March 22, 1865	Alabama	C	61st	1541
JACKSON, Curtis A.	January 2, 1865	Georgia	C	24th	1505
JACKSON, Henry A.	December 4, 1864	North Carolina	B	68th	884
JACKSON, Isaac	January 25, 1865	Virginia	B	42nd	1620
JACKSON, J.G.	August 12, 1864	South Carolina	E	4th Cavalry	133
JACKSON, J.W.	October 6, 1864	Kentucky	L	3rd	583
JACKSON, John	February 27, 1865	North Carolina	K	1st	2152
JACKSON, Joseph C.	November 12, 1864	North Carolina	C	11th	819
JACKSON, N. H.	February 11, 1865	North Carolina	A	36th	2094
JACKSON, R.	May 19, 1865	Virginia	E	2nd Artillery	2944
JACKSON, William M.	July 15, 1864	Georgia	C	53rd	Shohola
JACOBS, A.J.	November 1, 1864	South Carolina	A	21st	756
JACOBS, Jason	May 16, 1865	North Carolina	F	1st	2957
JAMES, Henry L.	September 21, 1864	North Carolina	G	43rd	338

Name	Date of Death	State	Company	Regiment/Notes	Woodlawn
JAMES, J. C.	March 16, 1865	Tennessee	B	1st Heavy Artillery	1694
JAMES, John B.	February 10, 1865	Virginia	I	11th	2080
JAMES, Marshall E.	November 22, 1864	North Carolina	E	2nd	935
JAMES, William J.	October 1, 1864	Georgia	B	12th	413
JARRATT, R.G.	October 1, 1864	Virginia	G	42nd	444
JEFFERS, George W.	March 27, 1865	Tennessee	C	31st Heavy Artillery	2497
JEFFRIES, John	March 10, 1865	North Carolina	E	35th - Corporal	1880
JENKINS, E. H.	March 21, 1865	Tennessee	I	14th	1551
JENKINS, Henry	March 13, 1865	North Carolina	K	5th	2429
JENKINS, R.O.	April 21, 1865	South Carolina	G	18th	1388
JENNINGS, C.M.	May 30, 1865	Virginia	F	29th	2909
*JERNEGAN, G.W.	February 12, 1865	North Carolina	E	20th - Corporal	2072
JERNIGAN, E. A.	October 6, 1864	North Carolina	H	50th	596
JERNIGAN, Lewis M.	December 28, 1864	North Carolina	H	20th	1297
JESSUP, William F.	July 9, 1865	Georgia	I	61st	2843
*JOB, Jesse R.	January 13, 1865	North Carolina	H	1st	1471
JOB, Jonathan F.	April 8, 1865	North Carolina	H	1st	2632
JOHNS, Decatur	September 9, 1864	Virginia	F	25th	201
JOHNS, Enoch	December 27, 1864	Florida	Jones Company	Florida Home Guards–1st Reserve	1290
JOHNSON, A. D.	March 30, 1865	Virginia	I	5th Cavalry	2535
JOHNSON, A.G.	April 13, 1865	Alabama	E	5th Reserve	2703
JOHNSON, Amos	April 10, 1865	North Carolina	B	36th	2721

Elmira Prison Camp

Name	Date of Death	State	Company	Regiment/Notes	Woodlawn
JOHNSON, Anderson	October 21, 1864	South Carolina	C	22nd	523
JOHNSON, Edward	September 12, 1864	North Carolina	G	5th – Sergeant	184
JOHNSON, H. A.	December 9, 1864	Alabama	B	59th	1034
JOHNSON, H. H.	March 13, 1865	Virginia	H	50th	1824
JOHNSON, J.	May 21, 1865	Virginia	B	50th Artillery	2938
JOHNSON, J.J.	February 16, 1865	South Carolina	G	25th	2210
*JOHNSON, J. L.	December 13, 1864	Louisiana	G	Power's Regiment	1125
JOHNSON, J.W.	February 13, 1865	Virginia		Carter's Battery	2045
JOHNSON, Larry	February 26, 1865	North Carolina	F	10th	2158
JOHNSON, M.P.	March 23, 1865	South Carolina	I	25th	2443
JOHNSON, Richard M.	February 20, 1865	North Carolina	C	36th	2332
JOHNSON, Robert F.	January 19, 1865	Georgia	F	9th	1204
JOHNSON, S. A.	February 23, 1865	North Carolina	C	36th	2257
JOHNSON, W. H.	February 16, 1865	Georgia	B	11th	2196
JOHNSON, William M. H.	January 18, 1865	North Carolina	K	52nd	1436
JOINCE, B.	March 4, 1865	Confederate States Navy		Steamship "Arrow" - Seaman	1968
JOINER, A.	July 15, 1864	Virginia	C	13th	Shohola
JOINER, J. R.	May 7, 1865	North Carolina	K	1st	2767
JOLLY, James R.	October 6, 1864	Virginia	H	60th	593
JONAS, Daniel	January 17, 1865	North Carolina	D	1st	1442
JONES, A. H.	January 22, 1865	North Carolina	I	1st	1598
JONES, A.J.	July 11, 1865	North Carolina	K	56th	2846

Name	Date of Death	State	Company	Regiment/Notes	Woodlawn
JONES, A. W.	November 17, 1864	North Carolina	I	1st	961
JONES, Alexander	March 29, 1865	North Carolina	F	18th	2522
JONES, B. B.	January 17, 1865	Georgia	E	7th - Corporal	1440
JONES, B. P.	April 1, 1865	North Carolina	B	40th - Sergeant	2583
JONES, C. A.	April 27, 1865	North Carolina	I	6th	2724
JONES, D.M.	October 10, 1864	South Carolina	H	7th Battalion	666
JONES, David	December 23, 1864	Virginia	A	42nd	1096
JONES, David W.	December 2, 1864	Virginia	H	5th	1009
JONES, George W.	September 7, 1864	Virginia	C	Alexander's Battery - Artillery	248
JONES, J.A.	February 26, 1865	South Carolina	L	21st	2122
JONES, J.B.	February 20, 1865	Alabama	C	1st Battalion of Artillery	2317
JONES, James M.	November 29, 1864	Alabama	F	1st Battalion of Artillery - Sergeant	985
JONES, John B.	May 10, 1865	Virginia	D	50th - Sergeant	2793
JONES, John L.	September 1, 1864	Alabama	B	61st	76
JONES, R.	July 15, 1865	North Carolina	C	1st	2875
JONES, W.H.	March 28, 1865	North Carolina	G	1st	2499
JONES, W.S.	March 10, 1865	Alabama	I	7th Cavalry	1853
JONES, William	October 28, 1864	North Carolina	C	51st	717
JONES, William A.	March 27, 1865	Virginia	I	53rd	2505
JONES, William A.	July 15, 1864	Virginia	D	22nd	Shohola
JONES, William T.	November 23, 1864	North Carolina	H	5th	920
JORDAN, A.	October 23, 1864	Georgia	G	7th Cavalry	865

Name	Date of Death	State	Company	Regiment/Notes	Woodlawn
JORDAN, A. C.	February 13, 1865	Georgia	A	24th - Corporal	2073
JORDAN, J. A.	March 7, 1865	North Carolina	I	32nd	2404
JORDAN, J.W.	September 22, 1864	South Carolina	F	6th - Corporal	486
JORDAN, James M.	February 26, 1865	Georgia	A	27th	1628
JORDAN, John J.	December 4, 1864	Virginia	F	44th - Sergeant	890
JORDAN, Kinyon	March 10, 1865	North Carolina	F	10th State Troop	1864
JORDAN, T.W.	February 15, 1865	Georgia	A	24th	2174
JORDAN, William H. H.	May 16, 1865	Georgia	K	12th	2960
JORDAN, William K.	September 16, 1864	South Carolina	I	21st	168
JOYNER, John F.	April 3, 1865	North Carolina	I	3rd Cavalry	2547
JOYNER, Samuel	February 28, 1865	North Carolina	E	36th, 2nd Artillery-State Troop	2148
JUDKINS, Joseph G.	October 11, 1864	Virginia	B	Hood's Battery	693
JUSTICE, Sparral	January 19, 1865	Virginia	B	42nd	1209
KALLAM, John N.	December 1, 1864	Virginia	F	46th	894
KAMP, J. A.	February 15, 1865	North Carolina	E	3rd - Corporal	2177
KANAN, James	March 27, 1865	Alabama	B	1st Artillery	2491
KAYLOR, John	March 27, 1865	North Carolina	B	35th	2500
KEANE, Edward	January 5, 1865	Alabama	A	21st - Drummer	1238
KEATON, Madison	December 20, 1864	Virginia	I	24th	1079
KEELER, J.	January 5, 1865	Georgia	H	24th	1258
KEEN, Moses H.	August 19, 1864	Florida	B	5th	117
KELLER, Noah	February 12, 1865	North Carolina	A	7th	2075

Name	Date of Death	State	Company	Regiment/Notes	Woodlawn
KELLEY, E.	October 25, 1864	Virginia		5th – Sergeant	710
KELLEY, J. M.	February 13, 1865	South Carolina	H	25th	2067
KELLEY, James	February 6, 1865	South Carolina	B	25th – Sergeant	1912
*KELLIHER, Dennis	December 24, 1864	Virginia	B	Baxton Artillery	1106
KELLUM, Reddin	November 24, 1864	North Carolina	B	24th	921
KELLY, J. C.	March 20, 1865	South Carolina	H	25th	2112
KELLY, Simon	February 16, 1865	South Carolina	C	21st	2202
KEMP, Edward	March 17, 1865	Alabama	E	1st Artillery	1697
KEMP, W. H.	September 2, 1864	South Carolina	C	22nd	211
KEMP, W. N.	February 14, 1865	Georgia	M	Phillips' Legion	2163
KENDALL, Samuel	December 13, 1864	North Carolina	K	42nd	1131
KENDRICK, W. P.	February 1, 1865	Virginia	H	42nd	1770
KENEDY, Thomas	March 2, 1865	Georgia	F	8th	2021
KENNEDY, A. J.	March 6, 1865	Virginia	I	26th Battalion	2394
KENNEDY, Levi B.	February 6, 1865	North Carolina	K	10th, 1st Artillery-State Troop	1893
KENNEDY, Lorenzo P.	February 2, 1865	Georgia	E	16th	1774
KENNEDY, William A.	April 12, 1865	North Carolina	A	32nd	2689
KENT, Richard	February 14, 1865	Texas	B	3rd	1739
KERNEZAY, Wesley	April 27, 1865	North Carolina	G	40th – Corporal	2725
KERR, Milton	February 13, 1865	North Carolina	A	51st	2036
KEY, D. S.	October 19, 1864	Virginia	H	34th	528
KEY, David	April 1, 1865	South Carolina	H	14th	2596

Alexander and Jackson Tew were brothers. James Martin Tew lived in Cumberland County and was a cousin of Alexander and Jackson Tew.

Jackson Tew enlisted first in Cumberland County, North Carolina and apparently Alexander and James Martin Tew went to Wilmington and enlisted on May 9, 1862.

Submitted by Jerome Tew.

Name	Date of Death	State	Company	Regiment/Notes	Woodlawn
KEY, R. R.	May 28, 1865	South Carolina	I	12th Corporal	2912
KEYS, Isaac	September 28, 1864	Virginia	A	26th	430
KIDD, Fields A.	September 13, 1864	Virginia	K	44th	271
KIDD, James M.	April 20, 1865	Georgia	C	35th	1381
KILBY, William	May 3, 1865	North Carolina	F	37th	2749
KILGORE, James	September 14, 1864	Georgia	C	9th – Hillyer Rifles	287
KILLINGSWORTH, James G.	March 20, 1865	Georgia	I	51st – Sergeant	1552
KIMBRO, William	September 29, 1864	Georgia	F	24th	427
KINEMORE, M.	September 29, 1864	South Carolina	D	18th	434
KING, A.	March 29, 1865	North Carolina	I	3rd	2510
KING, A.	October 21, 1864	North Carolina	D	8th	876
KING, B. S.	February 24, 1865	North Carolina	F	10th, 1st Artillery-State Troop	2252
KING, C.	April 18, 1865	Virginia	I	50th	1347
KING, C. B.	January 30, 1865	Alabama	A	1st Battalion of Artillery	1791
KING, Caswell	March 6, 1865	North Carolina	C	30th	2402
KING, E. P.	May 7, 1865	Georgia	H	13th	2769
KING, Henry W.	January 15, 1865	Virginia	B	29th	1449
KING, Hiram	December 5, 1864	Alabama	E	1st Battalion of Artillery	1031
KING, Hubard	March 26, 1865	North Carolina	G	45th	2473
KING, James	March 2/65	North Carolina	G	36th, 2nd Artillery-State Troop	2115
KING, Josiah	September 12, 1864	South Carolina	I	1st	174
KING, P.	March 16, 1865	Louisiana		Citizen of Louisiana	1695

Elmira Prison Camp

Name	Date of Death	State	Company	Regiment/Notes	Woodlawn
KING, Rufus	February 1, 1865	Alabama	F	15th	1773
KING, W.	June 3, 1865	South Carolina	E	25th	2818
KING, William	March 12, 1865	Virginia	K	50th	2427
KING, William T.	January 13, 1865	Florida	A	1st Reserve	1468
KINGSLOVER, A. F.	January 14, 1865	Virginia	I	48th	1459
KINLAW, Benjamin	April 16, 1865	North Carolina	K	40th, 3rd Artillery-State Troop	2720
*KINLAW, Neil	February 20, 1865	North Carolina	K	40th, 3rd Artillery-State Troop	2334
KINNEY, Clingman	October 21, 1864	North Carolina	I	8th	875
KIRBY, Dixon	April 13, 1865	North Carolina	K	10th	2770
KIRBY, James H.	September 12, 1864	Virginia	A	26th	181
KIRBY, James W.	October 10, 1864	Louisiana	B	7th	665
KIRBY, William H.	August 7, 1864	North Carolina	C	14th - Sergeant	13
KIRETT, F.	March 16, 1865	South Carolina	M	22nd	1709
KIRK, Joseph P.	September 15, 1864	Virginia	B	59th	299
KIRKLAND, J. William	December 8, 1864	Louisiana	B	Paine's Brigade	1171
KISER, George M.	March 27, 1865	North Carolina	H	5th	2524
KITCHIN, Thomas W.	April 12, 1865	Virginia	B	Hood's Battalion	2694
KITNER, John F.	September 19, 1864	North Carolina	A	52nd	327
KNIGHT, A. N.	September 15, 1864	Georgia		7th - Sergeant	290
KNIGHT, J.A.	February 22, 1865	Georgia	D	18th	2250
KNIGHT, John	January 24, 1865	Georgia	C	64th	1621
KNIGHT, John	April 15, 1865	North Carolina	C	3rd Battalion-Artillery	2714

Name	Date of Death	State	Company	Regiment/Notes	Woodlawn
KNIGHT, W.M.	November 16, 1864	Alabama	I	5th	955
KNODE, George W.	September 12, 1864	Virginia	C	2nd Cavalry	192
KNOTT, John H.	May 26, 1865	North Carolina	B	12th	2919
KNOWLES, John A.	May 21, 1865	North Carolina	E	36th	2937
KNOX, Gardner	February 28, 1865	North Carolina	C	2nd	2150
KNUCKLES, J.F.	September 21, 1864	Virginia	F	50th	337
KOLWICK, A.D.	December 17, 1864	Tennessee	A	1st Artillery	1735
KUESNER, John	February 14, 1865	Virginia	K	40th	2054
KYLE, James	November 20, 1864	North Carolina	K	11th	947
LADD, F.M.	March 14, 1865	South Carolina	F	Holcombe Legion	2189
LADD, G.W.	January 3, 1865	Virginia	G	55th	1260
LAFFLOON, G.	November 2, 1864	North Carolina	B	2nd	758
*LAFFMAN, William	November 29, 1864	North Carolina	F	37th	982
LAIL, Cicero	January 4, 1865	North Carolina	C	25th	1262
LAMAR, F.M.	January 25, 1865	Virginia	E	48th - Corporal	1625
LAMB, James	February 19, 1865	North Carolina	F	10th, 1st Artillery-State Troop	2335
LAMBERT, Green	December 28, 1864	Georgia	B	27th	1306
LAMBERT, S.	March 4, 1865	North Carolina	E	45th	1987
LAMBERTON, Eli	March 7, 1865	North Carolina	H	36th	2382
LANCE, Daniel	September 29, 1864	Virginia	H	25th	438
LANE, A.J.	February 25, 1865	North Carolina	D	32nd	2293
LANE, Henry	February 12, 1865	North Carolina	A	1st	2081

Name	Date of Death	State	Company	Regiment/Notes	Woodlawn
LANE, Robert J.	February 21, 1865	Virginia	B	44th	2232
LANGFORD, J.A.	February 6, 1865	Alabama	F	15th - Corporal	1922
LANGLEY, Charles W.	October 2, 1864	Virginia	B	10th	420
LANGLEY, J.R.	February 25, 1865	Georgia	H	16th	2285
LANIER, David	August 29, 1864	North Carolina	B	51st	58
LANIER, Francis M.	December 9, 1864	Florida	E	5th	1172
LANIER, Levi	January 13, 1865	North Carolina	D	3rd	1484
LANSDON, A.J.	February 20, 1865	Alabama	F	1st Battallion of Artillery	2318
LARBIN, Willis	March 18, 1865	North Carolina	H	36th	1728
*LARMAN, Joseph	February 18, 1865	North Carolina	E	2nd	2342
LARRICK, Joseph	October 1, 1864	Tennessee	G	63rd	417
LASHLEY, Lemuel	March 23, 1865	Alabama	G	3rd	2448
LAVANDER, Hy. L.	September 20, 1864	Virginia	A	4th	346
LAVANDER, Robert	February 8, 1865	Virginia	D	4th Cavalry	1937
LAWHON, James	April 11, 1865	North Carolina	A	36th	2670
LAWRENCE, A.	September 6, 1864	North Carolina	G	1st	240
LAWRENCE, James M.	April 23, 1865	North Carolina	F	36th	1403
LAWRENCE, John W.	December 3, 1864	Virginia	A	6th Cavalry	887
LAWRENCE, W.B.	March 4, 1865	North Carolina	G	1st	1986
LAWSON, J.W.	March 13, 1865	Georgia		Slaten's Company - Macon Light Artillery	2437
LAWSON, William	February 20, 1865	North Carolina	K	10th Artillery	2320

Looking west toward the Confederate monument from Davis Street.

Name	Date of Death	State	Company	Regiment/Notes	Woodlawn
LAXTON, Thomas W.	March 7, 1865	North Carolina	B	1st	2363
LEACH, Hugh	March 30, 1865	North Carolina	K	10th, 1st Artillery	2591
LEACH, W.	July 20, 1865	South Carolina	E	17th	2868
LEAR, William W.	February 6, 1865	Tennessee	D	1st Artillery	1903
LEATHERS, William L.	October 31, 1864	Louisiana	G	15th	738
LEE, Cyrus	April 23, 1865	Virginia	B	18th Cavalry	1398
LEE, David L.	September 20, 1864	North Carolina	E	51st	345
LEE, Harry	January 10, 1865	North Carolina	C	5th	1497
LEE, John H.	December 7, 1864	North Carolina	E	24th	1050
LEE, L. D.	May 15, 1865	Alabama	A	1st	2805
LEE, R. S.	February 26, 1865	Virginia	B	Hood's Battalion	2155
LEE, S. W.	July 15, 1864	North Carolina	K	8th	Shohola
LEE, William A.	September 20, 1864	Georgia	D	61st - Corporal	330
LEE, Z. N.	February 4, 1865	North Carolina	G	55th	1737
LEMMONS, James A	May 20, 1865	North Carolina	K	10th	2939
LEMON, William H.	January 8, 1865	Louisiana	C	3rd Cavalry	1220
LENTZ, John D.	February 18, 1865	North Carolina	C	42nd	2354
LENTZ, M.	September 18, 1864	North Carolina	C	18th	155
LEONARD, L. D.	March 7, 1865	North Carolina	B	45th	2380
LeQUEUX, William B.	September 6, 1864	South Carolina	I	27th	246
LESLIE, E.P.	February 24, 1865	North Carolina	K	1st	2272
LEWALLEN, B. F.	September 1, 1864	South Carolina	I	8th	71

Name	Date of Death	State	Company	Regiment/Notes	Woodlawn
LEWALLEN, G.M.	Decembr 19, 1864	Tennessee	A	1st Artillery	1069
LEWIS, Charles E.	August 25, 1864	Georgia	F	61st	107
LEWIS, D.	July 31, 1864	North Carolina	G	22nd	144
LEWIS, D. W.	March 18, 1865	South Carolina	A	2nd	1731
LEWIS, Edward S.	September 15, 1864	North Carolina	A	31st – Sergeant	303
LEWIS, G.	March 13, 1865	Georgia	G	7th Cavalry	1820
LEWIS, G.N.	February 6, 1865	Alabama	G	9th	1920
LEWIS, J.H.	October 19, 1864	North Carolina	H	38th	534
LEWIS, Nathan	September 24, 1864	North Carolina	E	18th	463
LEWIS, R. E.	March 16, 1865	Georgia	D	12th	1797
LEWIS, Willard	August 30, 1864	Virginia	B	Hood's Battalion	59
LEWIS, William H.	September 6, 1864	North Carolina	G	22nd	217
LIFARGE, F.M.	April 3, 1865	South Carolina	K	25th – Sergeant	2567
LIGHTNER, Thomas K.	December 5, 1864	Virginia	I	52nd	1019
LILES, H. H.	September 30, 1864	Georgia	G	7th Cavalry	406
LILLARD, Richard	September 27, 1864	North Carolina	G	45th	443
LILLEY, Joseph L.	November 24, 1864	North Carolina	F	31st	910
LIME, William	March 31, 1865	North Carolina	I	36th	2595
LINBECKER, C.M.	January 2, 1865	Texas	E	12th Cavalry	1338
*LINDSAY, E.H.	May 8, 1865	North Carolina	Confederate States Navy		2773
LINDSEY, Augustus	October 30, 1864	Georgia	O	Phillips' Legion	745
LINEBERGER, A. P.	September 21, 1864	North Carolina	C	28th	494

Name	Date of Death	State	Company	Regiment/Notes	Woodlawn
LINSAY, John W.	October 12, 1864	North Carolina	F	56th	572
LITCHFIELD, Joseph	April 29, 1865	North Carolina	B	8th	2733
LITTLE, Robert E.	March 20, 1865	North Carolina	D	13th Battery	1577
LITTLE, William P.	February 5, 1865	North Carolina	I	53rd	1896
LITTLEJOHN, S.	December 15, 1864	South Carolina	I	6th	1115
LIVELY, G.J.	August 30, 1864	South Carolina	K	Holcombe Legion	97
LOBLANE, Dosite	January 20, 1865	Louisiana	C	4th Cavalry	1201
LOCKAMORE, R.O.	August 21, 1864	Georgia	E	51st	110
LOCKENNA, R.	March 13, 1865	North Carolina	D	36th	2423
LOCKETT, James H.	November 15, 1864	Virginia	B	Hood's Battalion	803
LOCKRANA, D.	April 29, 1865	North Carolina	D	36th	2729
LOFTON, J.H.	March 30, 1865	North Carolina	G	40th	2534
LOGAN, F.	March 3, 1865	South Carolina	F	Holcombe Legion	1997
LOMAS, William	March 28, 1865	South Carolina	C	7th	2523
LONG, A.	April 22, 1865	North Carolina	E	35th	1394
LONG, Ezra	September 8, 1864	North Carolina	I	14th	94
LONG, John J.	March 22, 1865	North Carolina	C	18th	1510
LONG, Joseph	March 2, 1865	North Carolina	K	18th	2009
LONG, Joseph S.	December 9, 1864	North Carolina	H	33rd	1169
LONG, Robert	April 22, 1865	Virginia	B	10th	1393
LONG, S.P.	April 6, 1865	North Carolina	G	2nd	2629
LONG, Samuel	November 24, 1864	Tennessee	H	63rd	923

Name	Date of Death	State	Company	Regiment/Notes	Woodlawn
LONG, Virgil	August 5, 1864	Virginia	F	4th	142
LONG, W. E.	October 3, 1864	North Carolina	C	18th	612
LONGEST, John T.	January 5, 1865	Virginia	I	26th	1254
LORING, Joseph T.	March 12, 1865	Virginia	D	23rd	1847
LOUGHRY, Edward	March 15, 1865	Louisina	I	8th	1665
LOVE, H. S.	December 16, 1864	North Carolina	A	18th	1059
LOVELACE, William F.	November 25, 1864	North Carolina	G	22nd	909
LOVETT, J.M.	September 1, 1864	Georgia	B	7th Cavalry	88
LOVITT, H.	April 13, 1865	North Carolina	D	18th	2576
LOWE, James A.	March 11, 1865	Georgia	F	12th	1851
LOWE, John D.	May 3, 1865	Georgia	E	Cobb's Legion	2755
LOWE, William	September 5, 1864	North Carolina	D	24th	237
LOWRY, Calvin	August 30, 1864	South Carolina	K	6th - Corporal	96
LOYD, B.	October 20, 1864	North Carolina	G	28th	531
LOYD, James	December 30, 1864	North Carolina	I	1st	1323
LUCAS, J. F.	April 11, 1865	North Carolina	F	10th	2711
LUCAS, John H.	May 30, 1865	Virginia	D	5th - Corporal	2908
LUCKEY, David	February 28, 1865	North Carolina	G	52nd	2161
LUMLEY, William	October 11, 1864	North Carolina	G	7th	581
LUMPSFORD, Joseph A.	January 23, 1865	North Carolina	H	24th - Corporal	1612
LYLE, Henry H.	October 3, 1864	North Carolina	F	43rd	619
LYLE, James	December 10, 1864	South Carolina	D	17th	1154
LYNCH, Elijah	September 11, 1864	North Carolina	K	1st	252

Name	Date of Death	State	Company	Regiment/Notes	Woodlawn
LYNCH, G. W.	September 16, 1864	South Carolina	I	26th	296
LYNN, F. C.	December 12, 1864	Alabama	D	1st Battalion of Artillery	1142
LYNN, James W.	October 16, 1864	Virginia	G	12th Cavalry	560
LYONS, C. T.	March 2, 1865	Georgia	G	7th Cavalry	2017
MABE, Isaac	August 27, 1864	North Carolina	A	2nd - Sergeant	105
MABE, Samuel N.	May 1, 1865	Virginia	K	50th	2738
MABLEY, James H.	March 24, 1865	North Carolina	G	45th	2451
MABREE, J. B.	September 20, 1864	North Carolina	I	12th	331
MACE, Abraham	September 16, 1864	North Carolina	D	11th	305
MADDOX, Isham	February 28, 1865	Georgia	H	45th	2126
MADRAY, John L.	March 24, 1865	Georgia	E	Cobb's Legion	2445
MAHONES, A.	March 18, 1865	Tennessee	A	1st Artillery	1724
MALONE, Albert A.	August 28, 1864	North Carolina	I	45th - Sergeant	100
MALONE, P.	November 20, 1864	South Carolina	C	27th	941
MALPASS, O.M.	September 29, 1864	North Carolina	A	51st	431
MALPASS, T. D.	November 23, 1864	North Carolina	E	18th	990
*MANEY, O.H.	October 10, 1864	Virginia	G	6th	685
MANN, J. B.	February 26, 1865	North Carolina	G	40th	2157
MANN, N. R.	March 7, 1865	Virginia	C	42nd	2388
MANNIN, J. S.	February 1, 1865	North Carolina	H	33rd	1781
MANNING, Wallace	July 15, 1864	North Carolina	F	31st	Shohola
MARLER Joseph F.	February 25, 1865	North Carolina	F	28th	2292

Name	Date of Death	State	Company	Regiment/Notes	Woodlawn
MARLIN, Josephus	February 26, 1865	North Carolina	K	37th	2282
MARLOW, Nathan	January 9, 1865	North Carolina	A	3rd	1225
MARMADUKE, A.	October 1, 1864	Virginia	B	2nd	616
MARS, J. R.	October 9, 1864	North Carolina	D	45th	667
MARSHALL, J.N.	March 15, 1865	Virginia	I	10th	1688
MARSHALL, John H.	October 16, 1864	Virginia	G	26th	558
MARSHALL, R. A. M.	March 4, 1865	Virginia	A	6th – Corporal	1976
MARSHALL, Robert	September 9, 1864	Virginia	I	10th	200
MARSHALL, William	August 22, 1864	North Carolina	H	13th	29
MARTIN, Alfred	September 30, 1864	Texas	K	4th	401
MARTIN, Daniel B.	September 23, 1864	Virginia	C	24th	467
MARTIN, David	March 21, 1865	Louisiana	I	2nd	1530
MARTIN, G.W.	September 29, 1864	Georgia	C	7th Cavalry	439
MARTIN, J.	August 12, 1864	Alabama	H	59th	16
MARTIN, J.S.	November 29, 1864	Alabama	A	7th Cavalry	1003
MARTIN, John	October 24, 1864	Georgia	B	38th	711
MARTIN, R. C.	November 10, 1864	Georgia	H	7th Cavalry	828
MARTIN, Robert H.	August 23, 1864	North Carolina	E	51st	42
MARTIN, William H.	March 11, 1865	North Carolina	G	45th	1844
MARTIN, William H.	September 25, 1864	Georgia	D	12th	364
MASSEY, Abel C.	December 7, 1864	Georgia	G	14th – Corporal	1274
MASSEY, Joseph	January 23, 1865	Alabama	A	1st Battalion of Artillery	1596

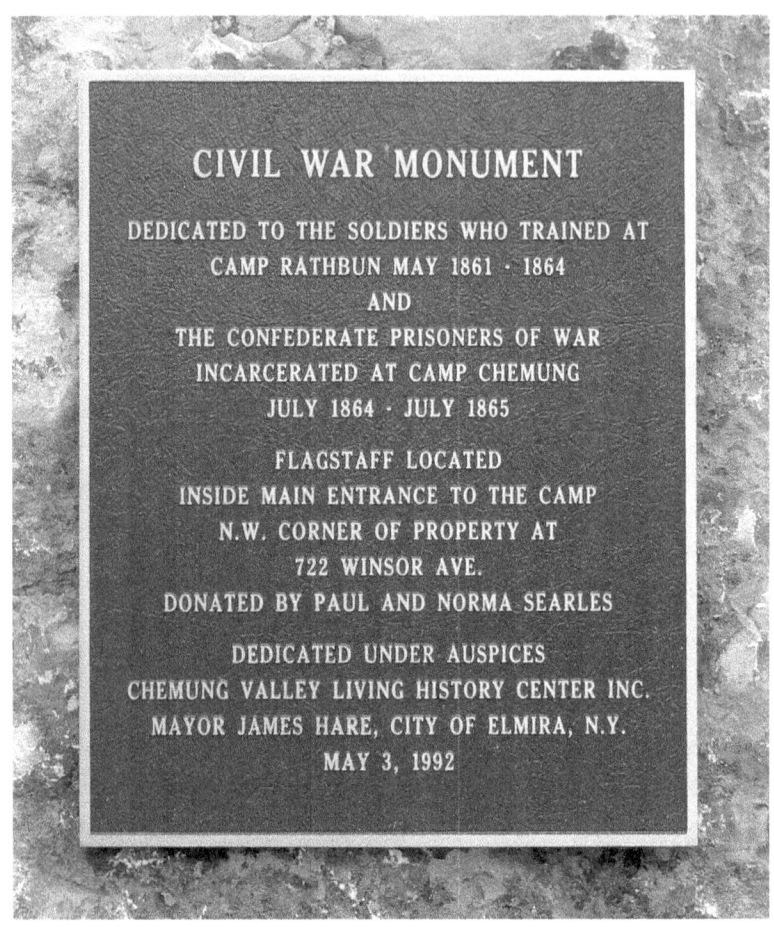

Civil War monument marker at the Barracks No. 3 Memorial on Winsor Avenue in Elmira.

Name	Date of Death	State	Company	Regiment/Notes	Woodlawn
MASSEY, S. E.	February 18, 1865	Georgia	H	16th – Sergeant	2343
MATHEWS, Archibald B.	February 10, 1865	North Carolina	E	40th	2090
MATHEWS, J.A.	May 2, 1865	South Carolina	H	18th	2743
MATHEWS, W.J.	April 7, 1865	South Carolina	H	25th	2649
MATHEWS, W. M.	September 15, 1864	South Carolina	K	18th	282
MATHEWS, William H.	March 27, 1865	North Carolina	C	36th	2471
MATHIAS, Elsy	December 29, 1864	North Carolina	G	1st	1308
MATTHEWS, Benjamin H.	April 8, 1865	Georgia	C	12th	2643
MATTHEWS, E.J.	March 17, 1865	North Carolina	C	36th	1555
MATTHEWS, J. M.	July 23, 1865	Virginia	A	52nd	2863
MATTHEWS, J.W.	May 23, 1865	Virginia	A	52nd	2928
MATTHEWS, Jacob W.	April 19, 1865	North Carolina	C	36th Battalion	1370
MATTHEWS, Joel	May 3, 1865	North Carolina	C	7th	2750
MATTHEWS, William	December 24, 1864	Florida		1st Reserves	1104
MAULDIN, James A.	January 8, 1865	Georgia	F	24th	1223
MAXWELL, John T.	October 30, 1864	Georgia	C	4th	733
MAXWELL, Whitford	March 11, 1865	North Carolina	D	36th	1835
MAY, Andrew	October 13, 1864	Virginia	D	14th Cavalry	699
MAY, John R.	November 29, 1864	Virginia	E	19th Cavalry	904
MAYFIELD, T.J.	September 19, 1864	Louisiana	K	2nd	504
MAYNARD, W.H.	February 5, 1865	North Carolina	C	47th	1904
MAYO, James	March 28, 1865	Virginia	D	5th Cavalry	2521

Name	Date of Death	State	Company	Regiment/Notes	Woodlawn
MAYS, Green J.	December 30, 1864	Louisiana	M	12th	1317
MAZE, G.W.	April 12, 1865	Virginia	K	50th	2695
MAZE, James M.	June 30, 1865	North Carolina	I	18th	2832
McALLISTER, E.	April 20, 1865	North Carolina	H	25th	1378
McANEAR, John	December 15, 1864	Alabama	H	12th	1113
McBRIDE, Alexander	February 18, 1865	North Carolina	G	45th – Sergeant	2345
McCALL, H. S.	October 10, 1864	South Carolina	E	4th Cavalry	680
McCALL, Neill	December 15, 1864	North Carolina	C	3rd	1063
McCANN, Andrew J.	March 12, 1865	Georgia	C	Cobb's Legion	2424
McCANN, Avery F.	December 6, 1864	Georgia	E	Cobb's Legion	1188
McCASKILL, James	March 18, 1865	North Carolina	G	40th	1553
McCLENNAN, P. C.	March 2, 1865	North Carolina	I	31st	2020
McCLENNAN, W. P.	October 11, 1864	South Carolina	F	Holcombe Legion - Sergeant	579
McCLENNAND, R.	November 21, 1864	Georgia	B	7th Cavalry	934
McCLENDON, F. P.	April 7, 1865	South Carolina	A	22nd	2654
McCLENDON, Joel	February 18, 1865	North Carolina	G	40th	2118
McCLOUD, John	February 3, 1865	North Carolina	H	3rd	1743
McCLOUD, Neal	December 10, 1864	North Carolina	E	3rd	1157
McCLURE, Nathaniel T.	January 1, 1865	Louisiana	A	1st	1333
McCOLLOM, Angus	August 14, 1864	North Carolina	D	49th	128
McCOMBS, M.B.	September 4, 1864	South Carolina	K	18th	73
McCORMICK, Duncan	July 21, 1865	North Carolina	E	40th, 3rd Artillery	2867

Name	Date of Death	State	Company	Regiment/Notes	Woodlawn
McCORQUADALE, Malcolm	July 15, 1864	North Carolina	I	51st	Shohola
McCRAW, William M.	February 2, 1865	Alabama	A	21st	1749
McCULLOUGH, John	August 15, 1864	South Carolina	B	14th	25
McCULLOUGH, Thomas	August 18, 1864	South Carolina	B	4th Cavalry - Corporal	121
McCULLOUGH, William A.	January 30, 1865	Tennessee	H	23rd	1784
McCURRY, M. Rufus	October 11, 1864	Georgia	C	Cobb's Legion	580
McCURVEY, T.W.	July 15, 1864	Georgia	K	16th	Shohola
McDANIEL, Charles	January 5, 1865	Louisiana	H	8th	1245
McDANIEL, W.M.	June 24, 1865	Georgia	F	24th	2881
McDANIEL, William	March 11, 1865	Alabama	I	12th	1846
McDANIELL, John	February 14, 1865	North Carolina	B	32nd	2169
McDONALD, D.K.	January 25, 1865	Florida	C	1st	1623
McDONALD, D.S.	March 23, 1865	Georgia	K	3rd	2442
McDONALD, Floyd	February 11, 1865	Virginia	I	16th Cavalry	2085
McDONALD, J.R,	June 11, 1865	South Carolina	I	21st	2885
McDONALD, John C.	May 1, 1865	Virginia	I	16th Cavalry	2735
McDONALD, Thomas	August 30, 1864	North Carolina	E	3rd	53
McDONOUGH, James	August 14, 1864	Virginia	B	12th Cavalry	126
McFENEY, Joseph	September 17, 1864	Virginia	A	63rd	313
McGAHEE, Samuel M.	May 4, 1865	Georgia	G	38th	2759
McGEE, Allison	October 1, 1864	North Carolina	B	2nd	411
McGEE, Isaac	December 12, 1864	North Carolina	I	37th	1130

Name	Date of Death	State	Company	Regiment/Notes	Woodlawn
McGEE, J.W.	September 16, 1864	Georgia	B	7th Cavalry	159
McGINSAY, John D.	September 4, 1864	North Carolina	F	3rd Cavalry	234
*McGOWEN, Daniel S.	December 9, 1864	South Carolina	B	17th	1151
McGREGOR, Adolphus	September 28, 1864	Georgia	B	15th	441
McGUIRE, William	March 21, 1865	Tennessee	B	1st	1535
McILWAIN, W. M.	January 2, 1865	South Carolina	F	Holcombe Legion	1345
McINTYRE, J.J.	March 5, 1865	South Carolina	F	21st - Sergeant Major	2413
McJOSH, Daniel	February 2, 1865	North Carolina	K	10th	2586
McKAY, Archibald P.	October 25, 1864	North Carolina	F	18th	736
McKENZIE, J.	February 10, 1865	Georgia	K	9th	1952
McKILLOP, John A.	December 27, 1864	North Carolina	A	25th - Sergeant	1296
McKINLEY, Stephen	December 26, 1864	Georgia	C	64th	1287
McKINNON, Robert	March 7, 1865	North Carolina	F	24th - Corporal	2396
McLANE, J.B.	May 10, 1865	South Carolina	E	11th	2792
McLAUGHLIN, R. W.	November 8, 1864	Virginia	E	31st	832
McLAUGHLIN, W.S	August 23, 1864	North Carolina	B	3rd	37
McLAURIN, John	February 13, 1865	North Carolina	G	40th	2065
McLEAN, Daniel	March 5, 1865	North Carolina	F	18th	1970
McLEAN, M.S.	February 5, 1865	North Carolina	F	18th - Sergeant	2557
McMANISS, T.M.	October 22, 1864	North Carolina	B	43rd	864
McMELLUN, Daniel J.	October 21, 1864	North Carolina	B	51st	874
McMELLAN, Peter	March 21, 1865	North Carolina	E	8th	1525

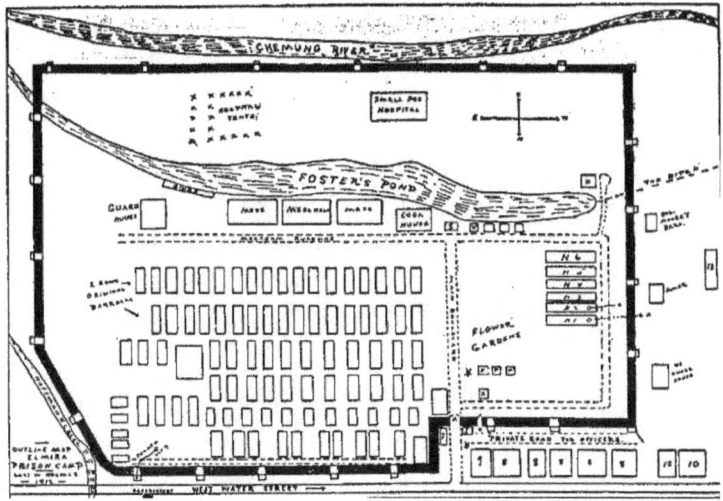

The top map was drawn by Clay Holmes, forty-five years after the camp's existence. If you put it over a current satellite view of the area, it does not quite line up perfectly, but you get the scope of its size.

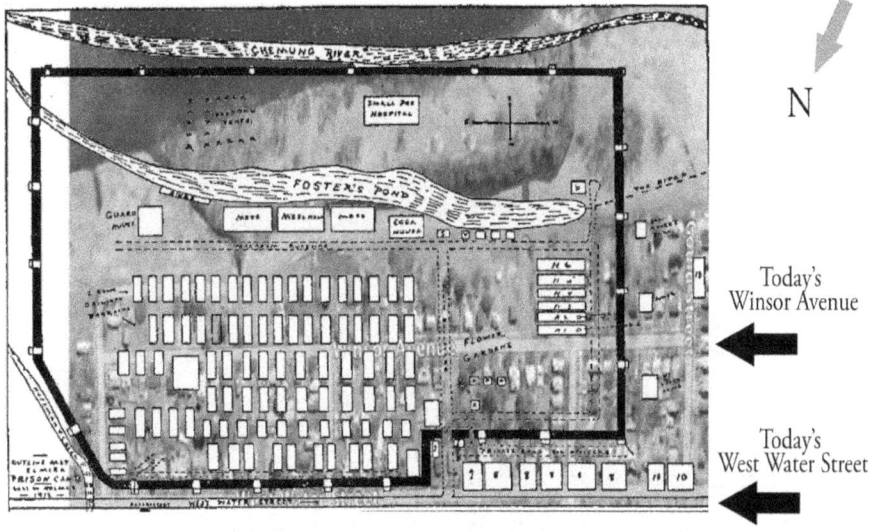

Today's Winsor Avenue

Today's West Water Street

Elmira Prison Camp

Name	Date of Death	State	Company	Regiment/Notes	Woodlawn
McMELLEN, Wafford W.	June 29, 1865	Georgia	K	24th	2827
McNAIR, Daniel P.	March 10, 1865	North Carolina	B	36th	1881
McNAIR, William A.	March 18, 1865	Alabama	F	1st Battalion of Artillery	1733
McNEAL, James A.	December 20, 1864	Alabama	E	1st Battalion of Artillery	1078
McNEESE, William T.	March 14, 1865	Florida	I	2nd	2433
McQUAQUE, A.	July 15, 1864	North Carolina	B	31st	Shohola
McQUEEN, D. M.	February 22, 1865	North Carolina	E	40th	2243
McRAE, V. A.	March 28, 1865	South Carolina	E	7th Cavalry	1856
McSWAIN, John E.	April 12, 1865	Alabama	E	13th	2696
*McWALTERS, John	April 11, 1865	South Carolina	D	17th	2676
*McWATTERS, John	November 9, 1864	South Carolina	D	17th	834
MEADOWS, Allen P.	October 19, 1864	Virginia	F	26th	529
MEADOWS, J.H.	March 11, 1865	North Carolina	I	5th	1863
MEADOWS, Ransom	October 20, 1864	North Carolina	C	3rd	524
MEADOWS, W. A.	March 16, 1865	Tennessee	C	44th	1686
MEDLIN, Daniel	February 3, 1865	South Carolina	C	7th - Corporal	1747
MEDLIN, Hawkins	May 23, 1865	North Carolina	I	1st	2930
MELLICHAMP, James M.	February 12, 1865	South Carolina	A	25th	2052
MELLOY, E.	April 19, 1865	North Carolina	D	1st	1369
MELTON, W. D. M.	October 10, 1864	North Carolina	C	21st	690
MELVIN, Daniel	March 17, 1865	North Carolina	I	36th	1716
MELVIN, William	March 18, 1865	North Carolina	H	36th	1710

Name	Date of Death	State	Company	Regiment/Notes	Woodlawn
MENINS, John	January 6, 1865	North Carolina	C	18th	1232
MERCER, C. G.	March 11, 1865	North Carolina	A	36th	1839
MERCER, F.	July 27, 1864	North Carolina	G	51st	149
MERCER, J. N.	March 17, 1865	North Carolina	A	36th	1696
*MEREDITH, John	May 6, 1865	North Carolina	D	7th	2373
MERRIAM, William	March 13, 1865	Alabama	C	1st Artillery	1823
MERRITT, John H.	January 9, 1865	Virginia	E	48th	1221
MERRITT, William	September 20, 1864	North Carolina	G	31st	342
METHVIN, Joseph C.	September 25, 1864	Georgia	H	64th	360
MEWMAN, Terrell	February 19, 1865	North Carolina	I	Thomas Legion	2348
MEYERS, Joseph E.	June 29, 1865	Virginia	F	52nd	2829
MIDDLETON, Martin V. B.	December 6, 1864	Alabama	E	1st Battalion of Artillery	1192
MIDLICOTT, S. R.	January 30, 1865	Virginia	C	24th Cavalry	1790
MILBY, H.	February 1, 1865	Virginia	H	26th	1776
MILBY, J. T.	May 21, 1865	Virginia	H	26th - Corporal	2935
MILLER, Alex	April 12, 1865	North Carolina	C	30th	2679
MILLER, Calhoun	February 10, 1865	North Carolina	A	57th	2084
MILLER, D. F.	August 24, 1864	North Carolina	H	5th	41
MILLER, E. C.	September 10, 1864	Tennessee	F	63rd	197
MILLER, Henry M.	February 3, 1865	Alabama	H	48th	1759
MILLER, Isaac A.	December 15, 1864	Virginia	C	11th	1116
MILLER, John	January 27, 1865	South Carolina	G	22nd	1648

Name	Date of Death	State	Company	Regiment/Notes	Woodlawn
MILLER, John F.	October 3, 1864	Virginia	I	52nd	623
MILLER, John H.	January 8, 1865	Virginia	K	2nd	1501
MILLER, Joseph	July 15, 1865	North Carolina	A	26th	2874
MILLER, N.	March 13, 1865	Florida		Florida Militia	1828
MILLER, Nathaniel	October 11, 1864	North Carolina	E	18th	694
MILLER, Samuel	June 28, 1865	Virginia	K	2nd	2825
MILLICAN, Francis O.	March 16, 1865	North Carolina	E	36th – Sergeant	1676
MILLS, F.B.	May 9, 1865	North Carolina	F	12th – Corporal	2781
MILLS, J.M.	February 13, 1865	Georgia	B	64th	2033
MILLS, M.J.	September 20, 1864	Arkansas	I	3rd	349
MILTON, John	April 12, 1865	Virginia	H	10th	2690
MINCE, J.R.	March 4, 1865	North Carolina	C	8th	2417
MINDEX, Enoch	February 10, 1865	North Carolina	H	36th	2666
MINER, Madison	November 14, 1864	North Carolina	H	5th	816
MINK, Calley	March 8, 1865	Virginia	B	48th	2384
MINOR, Jesse	January 28, 1865	Alabama	E	1st Battalion of Artillery	1809
MINOR, L.M.	February 14, 1865	Alabama	I	7th Cavalry - Sergeant	2167
MINTS, William	April 10, 1865	North Carolina	G	36th	2605
MISAMORE, Henry R.	December 13, 1864	North Carolina	D	42nd	1136
MITCHELL, B.	March 14, 1865	North Carolina	I	1st	1673
MITCHELL, George W.	September 7, 1864	South Carolina	L	1st Rifles	213
MITCHELL, J.W.	October 1, 1864	Virginia	I	50th	408

Name	Date of Death	State	Company	Regiment/Notes	Woodlawn Shohola
MITCHELL, Joseph	July 15, 1864	Virginia	B	42nd	740
MITCHELL, M.C.	October 31, 1864	Virginia	F	26th	1039
MITCHELL, Samuel	December 10, 1864	Georgia	H	44th	1850
MITCHELL, William A.	March 11, 1865	Alabama	G	10th	2772
MITCHEN, E.E.	May 7, 1865	Georgia	I	7th Cavalry	2799
MITCHEN, Samuel D.	May 13, 1865	Virginia	A	58th - Sergeant	2185
MIXON, A.W.	February 14, 1865	South Carolina	I	25th	2682
MIXON, Green	April 11, 1865	Alabama		1st Battalion of Artillery	1002
MIXON, Harvey	November 30, 1864	Louisiana	F	9th	2774
MOCK, Henry A.	May 8, 1865	North Carolina	F	13th	679
MOFFATT, Veno	October 11, 1864	North Carolina	F	24th	1068
MONEYMAKER, John	December 18, 1864	Virginia	H	25th	2472
MONGLE, Abram F.	March 26, 1865	Virginia	I	48th	1895
MONTGOMERY, P.C.	February 5, 1865	North Carolina	H	33rd	2355
MONTGOMERY, W.K.	February 19, 1865	Virginia	E	50th	578
MOODY, James E.	October 11, 1864	North Carolina	C	61st	998
MOON, William	November 29, 1864	North Carolina	F	22nd	2648
MOONEY, Zilman	April 6, 1865	North Carolina	E	45th	2607
MOORE, B.F.	April 10, 1865	South Carolina	B	21st	1325
MOORE, Calvin	December 31, 1864	Virginia	F	47th	620
MOORE, George H.	October 3, 1864	North Carolina	I	37th	130
MOORE, Isaac	August 12, 1864	Virginia	B	36th	

Memorial Day at Woodlawn National Cemetery. The cemetery is a very peaceful, quiet place with beautiful landscaping.

Name	Date of Death	State	Company	Regiment/Notes	Woodlawn
MOORE, J.J.	February 17, 1865	South Carolina	A	21st	2213
MOORE, J.W.	August 15, 1864	North Carolina	G	45th	9
MOORE, James R.	August 13, 1864	Virginia	A	46th	19
MOORE, James R.	July 18, 1865	North Carolina	D	21st	2872
MOORE, John A.	January 10, 1865	Georgia	H	Cobb's Legion	1215
MOORE, L.	January 30, 1865	Virginia	I	25th Cavalry	1803
MOORE, William H.	February 28, 1865	North Carolina	G	40th	2151
MOORE, William T.	February 4, 1865	Georgia	L	Phillips' Legion	1738
MOOTSHEARD, J.W.	October 13, 1864	Virginia	H	26th	695
MORAGUE, Augustus W.	October 31, 1864	Virginia	G	10th - Sergeant	742
MORGAN, Daniel M.	January 29, 1865	Georgia	C	18th - Sergeant	1812
MORGAN, Elwood	April 26, 1865	North Carolina	B	45th	1419
MORGAN, J.N.	February 21, 1865	North Carolina	E	5th	2233
MORGAN, John N.	August 20, 1864	Florida	D	5th	114
MORRELL, B.P.	February 2, 1865	Georgia	E	7th Cavalry	1760
MORRIS, C.M.	September 13, 1864	North Carolina	B	31st	176
MORRIS, Martin V.	November 18, 1864	Virginia	K	26th	972
MORRIS, Richard C.	September 20, 1864	Virginia	D	44th	328
MORRIS, S.A.	December 8, 1864	North Carolina	C	1st	1170
MORRIS, Thomas	November 13, 1864	North Carolina	E	8th	822
MORRIS, Walter C.	February 15, 1865	Georgia	C	3rd Battalion-Sharpshooters	2173
MORRISON, Lewis W.	November 30, 1864	North Carolina	G	38th - Sergeant	1001

Name	Date of Death	State	Company	Regiment/Notes	Woodlawn
MORROW, W.M.	December 12, 1864	Louisiana		Citizen of Louisiana	1138
MORSE, J.P.	September 2, 1864	South Carolina	H	22nd	85
MORSE, John W.	August 5, 1864	North Carolina	G	45th	8
MORTON, William P.	December 11, 1864	North Carolina	I	8th	1150
MOSS, Wiley I.	December 4, 1864	Georgia	D	3rd Battalion	881
MOTES, Patrick H.	December 23, 1864	Alabama	E	1st Battalion of Artillery	1100
MOUNTAIN, William R.	April 18, 1865	Alabama	C	61st	1357
MOWRY, Ephraim	February 4, 1865	Virginia	G	2nd	2553
MULL, John M.	June 20, 1865	North Carolina	F	55th	2810
MULLENS, M.G.	February 26, 1865	Tennessee	G	17th	2146
MULLIGAN, W.H.	January 26, 1865	South Carolina	E	11th	1634
MULLIN, G.W.	May 24, 1865	North Carolina	G	49th	2925
MUNROE, Duncan	July 15, 1864	North Carolina	I	51st	Shohola
MURPHY, J.W.	February 21, 1865	North Carolina	C	33rd	2235
MURPHY, L.D.	February 28, 1865	South Carolina	H	25th	2134
MURPHY, Marshall	October 3, 1864	Virginia	A	25th	610
MURRAY, Henry	February 2, 1865	South Carolina	H	11th	1771
MURRAY, Henry G.	September 18, 1864	North Carolina	E	31st	510
MURRAY, J.W.	December 1, 1864	North Carolina	I	8th	1013
MURWARDY, Charles D.	December 21, 1864	Louisiana		Citizen of Louisiana	1081
MUSE, C.G.	May 11, 1865	North Carolina	I	2nd - Corporal	2794
MYERS, C. C.	August 2, 1864	Virginia	I	26th Battalion	147

Name	Date of Death	State	Company	Regiment/Notes	Woodlawn
MYRICH, Robert N.	September 19, 1864	Virginia	G	3rd	496
MYRICK, G.W.	February 3, 1865	Virginia	C	51st	1765
MYRICK, John F.	February 16, 1865	Alabama	E	61st – Corporal	2199
MYRICK, Josiah	April 18, 1865	Alabama	E	1st Battalion of Artillery	1349
MYRICK, N.T.	December 5, 1864	Virginia	G	3rd	1027
MYRICK, W.H.	April 25, 1865	Virginia	G	26th	1416
NANCE, Joseph W.	October 25, 1864	North Carolina	F	28th – Corporal	851
NAYLOR, Columbus	December 19, 1864	Texas	K	1st Cavalry	1070
*NEAL, W.C.	February 23, 1865	South Carolina	DH	17th	1397
NEIGHBORS, William	October 3, 1864	South Carolina	G	27th	631
NEIGHBOURS, Joshua	November 29, 1864	North Carolina	E	42nd	997
NEILL, John L.	November 25, 1864	Tennessee	E	23rd	918
NELSON, J.	January 15, 1865	Alabama	F	1st Battalion of Artillery	1454
NELSON, John H.	November 2, 1864	Alabama	E	44th	844
NELSON, William A.	August 30, 1864	Virginia	E	25th Battalion	54
NESSE, W.	April 12, 1865	Georgia	C	16th	2706
NETHERLY, Robert T.	October 12, 1864	North Carolina	I	8th – Sergeant	570
NEVILL, J. H.	February 24, 1865	North Carolina	K	1st	1412
NEVILL, R. H.	March 19, 1865	North Carolina	G	12th	1580
NEWELL, J.G.	February 18, 1865	North Carolina		Citizen of North Carolina	1352
NEWELL, James A.	October 5, 1864	North Carolina	E	45th	644
NEWMAN, James H.	December 21, 1864	Virginia	A	58th	1736

Elmira Prison Camp

Name	Date of Death	State	Company	Regiment/Notes	Woodlawn
NEWMAN, Joseph	September 12, 1864	Virginia	K	50th	191
NEWMAN, Thomas	May 20, 1865	Virginia	A	58th	2942
NICHOLS, Hazard	March 20, 1865	North Carolina	K	10th	1579
NICHOLS, Isaac	January 21, 1865	South Carolina	A	7th Battalion	1587
NICHOLS, J.A.	September 24, 1864	North Carolina	K	53rd	466
NICHOLSON, W.J.	March 9, 1865	North Carolina	H	22nd	1876
NIFONG, Madison	September 28, 1864	North Carolina	G	2nd	437
NIXON, Harvey	November 23, 1864	North Carolina	A	1st	929
NOBLES, J.E.	February 11, 1865	Virginia	F	26th	2074
NOBLES, R.J.	March 10, 1865	Alabama	F	12th	1854
NOLL, John	October 14, 1864	Virginia	F	50th	700
NORRIS, J.C.	January 6, 1865	Georgia	A	7th Cavalry	1242
NORTH, James P.	December 24, 1864	Virginia	H	14th	1109
NORVILLE, J. S.	November 22, 1864	North Carolina	I	35th	927
NOWELL, W. N.	August 29, 1864	North Carolina	H	31st	57
NUSMAN, M.J.	March 28, 1865	North Carolina	H	8th	2494
O'BRIEN, Edward	October 2, 1864	North Carolina	F	8th – Sergeant	621
O'BRYANT, William	March 8, 1865	North Carolina	A	24th	2366
O'ROARKE, John	December 14, 1864	Virginia	I	26th Battalion	1120
O'NEAL, James	March 5, 1865	Florida		Norwood's Home Guard	2418
OAKS, James	November 9, 1864	Tennessee	I	44th	782
ODEN, William W. W.	January 30, 1865	Alabama	E	1st Battalion of Artillery	1799

The Shohola monument commemmorates the fifty-two prisoners who died in the Shohola, Pennsylvania train wreck in July 1864. The prisoners were destined for Elmira when their train hit another train head-on in Shohola. In 1911, the victims were disinterred from Shohola and brought to Elmira.

Name	Date of Death	State	Company	Regiment/Notes	Woodlawn
ODOM, Alfred	November 20, 1864	North Carolina	F	32nd	949
ODOM, J. H.	January 4, 1865	Alabama	A	1st Battalion of Artillery-Corporal	1251
ODOM, J.J.	February 25, 1865	Alabama	A	1st Battalion of Artillery-Sergeant	2276
ODOM, John H.	October 11, 1864	Georgia	B	35th	577
ODUM, H. A.	October 24, 1864	Alabama	G	12th	862
OGLESBEY, B. F.	March 28, 1865	Virginia	C	26th	2495
OGLESBY, Richard	September 14, 1864	Virginia	G	26th	503
OLIVER, J.H.	March 1, 1865	North Carolina	I	3rd	2106
OLIVER, Peter	March 19, 1865	North Carolina	D	45th	1729
ORICE, Robert T.	February 13, 1865	North Carolina	B	36th	2066
ORISON, Jonah	October 14, 1864	Virginia	K	6th Cavalry	599
OTT, William E.	March 5, 1865	South Carolina	G	25th	1981
OTTAWAY, R. M.	May 5, 1865	North Carolina	G	36th	2762
OTTERS, Cooney	December 24, 1865	North Carolina	B	53rd	1611
OTWELL, Jesse R.	October 4, 1864	North Carolina	H	1st	638
OUTLAW, John L.	March 28, 1865	North Carolina	C	3rd Light Artillery	2511
OVERSTREET, J.M.	June 6, 1865	Virginia	F	34th	2893
*OWENS, D.	September 12, 1864	South Carolina	A	5th	178
OWENS, Harbin	October 10, 1864	North Carolina	F	3rd	683
OWENS, Henry	January 7, 1865	South Carolina	C	22nd	1500
OWENS, J.C.	March 30, 1865	North Carolina	B	54th	2540
OWENS, J.P.	August 22, 1864	Georgia		Light Artillery	34

Name	Date of Death	State	Company	Regiment/Notes	Woodlawn
OWENS, John	February 26, 1865	Virginia	I	50th	2283
OWENS, John O.	February 16, 1865	North Carolina	E	53rd	2209
OWENS, Joseph	August 28, 1864	North Carolina	I	22nd	46
OWENS, L. H.	April 19, 1865	North Carolina	I	36th	1367
OWENS, Samuel	February 21, 1865	South Carolina	A	21st	2301
OWENS, T. A.	October 10, 1864	South Carolina	C	22nd	669
OWENS, W. H.	March 21, 1865	South Carolina	K	25th	1537
OWENS, William	November 29, 1864	South Carolina	C	22nd	987
OWENS, Williams	April 26, 1865	South Carolina	C	22nd	1424
OYLER, T. B.	January 23, 1865	North Carolina	H	32nd	1606
PACE, Samuel S.	August 20, 1864	Georgia	D	57th	109
PACK, Robert L.	October 3, 1864	Virginia	G	26th	630
PADEN, Andrew W.	April 3, 1865	Georgia	C	Cobb's Legion	2569
PADGETT, A. J.	September 12, 1864	North Carolina	I	3rd State Troop	180
PADGETT, F. L.	November 2, 1864	Florida	K	10th	751
PAGE, Bennett	March 7, 1865	North Carolina	G	36th	2400
PAGE, J.R.	April 1, 1865	Georgia	C	16th	2584
PAITING, John	March 10, 1865	North Carolina	B	36th	1865
PALMER, F.M.	September 22, 1864	Alabama	D	6th	491
PARKER, B. B.	July 12, 1865	South Carolina	E	21st - Sergeant	2847
PARKER, Benjamin F.	December 5, 1864	North Carolina	B	24th State Troop	1020
PARKER, Irwin	February 21, 1865	South Carolina	F	41st	2310

Name	Date of Death	State	Company	Regiment/Notes	Woodlawn
PARKER, J. R.	June 17, 1865	North Carolina	G	36th	2808
*PARKER, James P.	September 18, 1864	North Carolina	K	23rd	156
PARKER, M.	April 11, 1865	North Carolina	B	31st	2691
PARKER, Nathaniel W.	February 5, 1865	Georgia	K	12th	1649
PARKS, Britton	April 1, 1865	North Carolina	K	28th	2573
PARKS, Henry D.	January 19, 1865	Alabama	A	1st Battalion of Artillery	1433
PARKS, J.C.	July 15, 1864	Virginia	H	22nd	Shohola
PARKS, Samuel S.	January 4, 1865	Georgia	C	Cobb's Legion	1252
PARKS, William	September 27, 1864	North Carolina	E	42nd	381
PARRISH, A.J.	March 21, 1865	Virginia	B	44th	1543
PARRISH, Joseph W.	September 22, 1864	Virginia	D	44th	493
PARRISH, T.M.	June 17, 1865	Alabama	A	21st	2877
PARROTT, J.M.	July 16, 1865	South Carolina	B	21st	2873
*PATE, Able	May 5, 1865	Georgia	F	19th	2421
PATE, Asa	April 2, 1865	North Carolina	F	10th	2580
PATE, Daniel	May 9, 1865	North Carolina	K	40th	2782
PATE, Drury	October 31, 1864	Alabama	K	5th	744
PATE, James E.	March 19, 26, 1865	North Carolina	K	40th	2466
PATRICK, J. N.	July 15, 1864	Virginia	H	26th	Shohola
PATRICK, James	January 6, 1865	Virginia	D	50th	1240
PATRICK, R. C.	February 5, 1865	South Carolina	F	18th	1918
PATTERSON, John W.	December 30, 1864	Georgia	C	35th	1312

Name	Date of Death	State	Company	Regiment/Notes	Woodlawn
PATTERSON, W.T.	May 10, 1865	North Carolina	H	56th	2789
PATTERSON, William H.	September 26, 1864	North Carolina	K	7th	454
PATTON, H.P.	January 27, 1865	Virginia	H	50th	1649
PATTON, James W.	November 8, 1864	Maryland	F	1st	829
PATTS, M.P.	April 10, 1865	Georgia	I	30th	2615
PAYNE, Archie	December 4, 1864	Alabama	F	1st Battalion of Artillery	883
PAYNE, Cary J.	February 2, 1865	North Carolina	A	25th	1754
PAYTON, Frank	August 11, 1864	Virginia	D	7th	15
PAYTON, John H.	January 21, 1865	Georgia	A	24th	1584
PEACOCK, George W.	January 8, 1865	South Carolina	G	7th Cavalry	1229
PEACOCK, Jacob	September 4, 1864	North Carolina	G	2nd	232
PEAL, A.D.	September 20, 1864	South Carolina	D	5th	344
PEAL, R.H.	October 12, 1864	North Carolina	K	33rd	568
PEARSON, Anthony	October 16, 1864	South Carolina	C	22nd	552
PEARSON, Samuel J.	September 24, 1864	South Carolina	C	22nd	461
PEARSON, Stanford	November 6, 1864	North Carolina	I	32nd	846
PECK, Eli	October 7, 1864	North Carolina	H	8th	594
PECK, William H.	December 31, 1864	Virginia	H	26th - Corporal	1321
PEDY, S.H.	March 30, 1865	Virginia	F	42nd	2542
PEEL, James	April 4, 1865	North Carolina	G	40th, 3rd Artillery	2554
PEIKS, J.D.	July 15, 1864	Virginia	E	47th	Shohola
PENCE, Harrison	August 12, 1864	South Carolina	F	2nd	18

Name	Date of Death	State	Company	Regiment/Notes	Woodlawn
PENNELL, Calvin	March 19, 15, 1865	North Carolina	D	40th	1664
PENNY, W.J.	January 22, 1865	North Carolina	H	51st	1605
PEOPLES, Martin V.	October 10, 1864	North Carolina	C	8th	668
PERDIEUX, C.	June 21, 1865	South Carolina	E	21st	2812
PERDUE, Charles	March 19, 22, 1865	North Carolina	G	40th, 3rd Artillery	1539
PERKINS, W.L.	March 19, 28, 1865	North Carolina	B	1st	2507
PERRINGER, Hy	September 2, 1864	North Carolina	H	8th	79
PERRY, Hiram N.	April 2, 1865	North Carolina	G	40th	2578
PERRY, J.H.	July 6, 1865	North Carolina	B	13th	2838
PERRY, John C	March 19, 20, 1865	North Carolina	B	36th	1562
PERRY, Presley	August 9, 1864	South Carolina	E	22nd	138
PERVIS, Henry	February 12, 1865	South Carolina	K	21st	2057
*PERYMORE, L. B.	March 19, 18, 1865	Alabama	A	1st Artillery	1708
PETERS, Joseph B.	December 22, 1864	Virginia	A	25th - Sergeant	1086
PETERSON, Haywood L.	November 12, 1864	North Carolina	E	18th - Corporal	780
PETERSON, John	February 14, 1865	North Carolina	E	51st	2034
PETSEY, Henderson S.	September 3, 1864	Virginia	D	14th Cavalry	72
PETTICORD, George	December 7, 1864	North Carolina	G	2nd	1177
PHELPS, Elisha	September 4, 1864	North Carolina	A	15th	228
PHILAND, Joseph	January 28, 1865	North Carolina	D	32nd	1643
PHILEN, Robert D.	November 15, 1864	Alabama	E	61st	821
PHILLIPS, Bryan	April 8, 185	North Carolina	G	40th, 3rd Artillery	2633

Name	Date of Death	State	Company	Regiment/Notes	Woodlawn
PHILLIPS, E.	February 20, 1865	South Carolina	A	21st	2328
PHILLIPS, James	April 10, 1865	Virginia	H	5th	2608
PHILLIPS, Jeremiah	March 19, 1, 1865	Mississippi	K	42nd	2102
PHILLIPS, John	February 6, 1865	South Carolina	A	21st	1916
PHILLIPS, Nelson	December 21, 1864	Tennessee	D	7th	1083
PHILLIPS, Wyley	March 15, 1865	Georgia	H	7th Cavalry	1689
PHILYAN, A. H.	April 26, 1865	Alabama	E	5th	1421
PHIPPS, David	September 3, 1864	North Carolina	K	37th	68
PHIPPS, J. E.	May 7, 1865	North Carolina	B	45th	2768
PICKARD, John	April 24, 1865	North Carolina	D	53rd	1411
PICKERING, Wesley H.	December 2, 1864	Tennessee	F	3rd	1011
PICKETT, James	September 2, 1864	Alabama	H	44th	86
PIERCE, Taylor	February 8, 1865	Louisiana	B	1st - Nelligan's Infantry	1928
PIERCE, W.J.	August 1, 1864	Louisiana	D	18th - Corporal	143
PINKARD, John M.	December 13, 1864	Louisiana	G	8th	1128
PINSON, William	December 17, 1864	Louisiana	A	1st Cavalry	1271
PITCHFORD, R.D.	July 15, 1864	North Carolina	E	1st Cavalry	Shohola
PITTS, D.W.	November 15, 1864	Alabama	F	1st Battalion of Artillery	799
PLOWDEN, John Covert	May 3, 1865	South Carolina	I	25th	2754
POELLNITZ, S.C.	December 21, 1864	Alabama	C	21st	1085
POFF, Thomas	December 2, 1864	Virginia	B	4th	895
POLK, L.M.	February 15, 1865	Georgia	I	24th	2166

Memorial Day, looking east toward Davis Street.

Name	Date of Death	State	Company	Regiment/Notes	Woodlawn
POLSTON, James W.	April 19, 1865	Alabama	A	1st Battalion of Artillery	1374
POOLE, George	October 14, 1864	North Carolina	H	3rd Cavalry	706
POOLE, Henson	March 27, 1865	Virginia		Citizen of Virginia	2513
POOLE, James F.	December 7, 1864	North Carolina	I	33rd	1193
POOLE, Quentine R.	October 3, 1864	North Carolina	D	31st	625
POPE, C.T.	December 6, 1864	Alabama	B	7th Cavalry	1190
POPE, D.W.	July 15, 1864	North Carolina	I	51st	Shohola
POPE, John N.	June 5, 1865	Georgia	G	8th – Corporal	2894
POPE, William A.	January 22, 1865	North Carolina	K	1st	1604
POSTING, F.	April 26, 1865	Virginia	D	30th	1425
POTTER, R.H.	April 9, 1865	North Carolina	B	36th	2613
POTTER, Thomas N.	September 13, 1864	Georgia	G	16th	269
POTTS, Calvin J.	January 5, 1865	North Carolina	B	46th	1261
POTTS, James W.	April 6, 1865	Alabama	K	3rd	2658
POUND, Jacob A.	February 13, 1865	North Carolina	G	36th	2051
POWE, James F.	May 15, 1865	South Carolina	D	21st	2764
POWE, Joseph E.	March 8, 1865	South Carolina	D	21st	2364
POWELL, A. Louis	August 14, 1864	South Carolina	C	22nd	127
POWELL, E.	June 23, 1865	South Carolina	H	25th	2815
POWELL, George L.	November 28, 1864	North Carolina	F	3rd Artillery	993
POWELL, J.M.	February 22, 1865	Virginia		Carter's Battery	2251
POWELL, James E.	January 11, 1865	Louisiana	A	3rd Cavalry	1493

Name	Date of Death	State	Company	Regiment/Notes	Woodlawn
POWELL, Jeremiah	November 10, 1864	Georgia	K	12th	767
POWELL, John	January 31, 1865	Virginia	A	60th	1788
POWELL, John J.	February 19, 1865	Louisiana		Citizen of Louisiana	2338
POWELL, John W.	September 9, 1864	North Carolina	H	32nd	206
POWELL, N.P.	February 25, 1865	Virginia	E	59th Battalion	2288
POWELL, William W.	March 17, 1865	North Carolina	D	32nd	1704
POWERS, George	April 12, 1865	South Carolina	G	27th	2677
POWERS, William	January 25, 1865	Virginia	K	48th	1614
PRATER, P.M.	December 18, 1864	South Carolina	D	14th	1067
PRATT, Thomas A.	January 15, 1865	Virginia	D	26th	1453
PRESLEY, E.B.	February 28, 1865	Alabama	A	1st Battalion of Artillery	2131
PRESLEY, J.A.	February 10, 1865	Alabama	A	1st Battalion of Artillery	2088
PRESSON, John J.	February 17, 1865	Virginia	B	Hood's Battalion	2336
PRESTGRAVES, Richard	January 19, 1865	Virginia		Citizen of Virginia	1207
*PREVETT, Abner	July 5, 1864	North Carolina	I	4th – State Troop	2855
PREWATT, E.	December 13, 1864	North Carolina	E	51st	1141
PRICE, Alex J.	October 10, 1864	Alabama	K	6th	686
PRICE, Jackson	September 25, 1864	North Carolina	H	32nd	359
PRICE, James G.	January 3, 1865	Virginia	G	4th – Corporal	1334
PRICE, John	September 18, 1864	South Carolina	K	18th	314
PRICE, John	November 2, 1864	North Carolina	E	37th	575

Name	Date of Death	State	Company	Regiment/Notes	Woodlawn
PRIDGEON, M.	April 15, 1865	North Carolina	D	36th	2713
PRINCE, Berryman	April 25, 1865	South Carolina	B	2nd - Rifles	1413
PRIVITT, Samson C.	January 1, 1865	North Carolina	B	37th	1330
PRUDEN, John W.	December 26, 1864	Virginia	F	61st	1270
PURCELL, Duncan	April 10, 1865	North Carolina	C - State Troop	36th, 2nd Artillery	2668
PURCELL, Thomas	April 11, 1865	Alabama	F	1st Battalion of Artillery	2688
PURCER, Benjamin	April 5, 1865	Alabama	F	1st Battalion of Artillery	2544
PYNER, J.	March 4, 1865	North Carolina	E	3rd	1964
QUARLES, W.O.	October 1, 1864	Alabama	H	3rd	414
QUICK, James E.	March 7, 1865	North Carolina	A - Lenoir Braves	3rd Quarter Mstr. Sergeant	1967
QUINN, Jesse	April 18, 1865	North Carolina	I	18th Quarter Mstr. Sergeant	1350
RABB, Benjamin F.	January 13, 1865	Alabama	C	1st Battalion of Artillery	1474
RAINS, Henry	April 17, 1865	Virginia	C	53rd	1354
RAINWATER, J. W.	October 21, 1864	South Carolina	E	4th Cavalry	526
RAMSEY, Benjamin E.	March 28, 1865	Virginia	E	34th	2365
RAMSEY, William J.	November 9, 1864	Alabama	G	41st	789
RANDALL, Robert D.	February 12, 1865	Georgia	D	2nd Battalion	2071
RANDOLPH, William T.	January 13, 1865	Virginia	F	6th	1457
RANEY, J.R.	September 6, 1864	North Carolina	D	42nd	220
RANEY, Mark	September 14, 1864	Georgia	D	64th	292
RANKIN, Anthony	April 18, 1865	Alabama	F	1st Battalion of Artillery	1362
RANKIN, William	January 30, 1865	South Carolina	E	1st Rifles	1785

Name	Date of Death	State	Company	Regiment/Notes	Woodlawn
RAUTLEY, Kenyon	February 10, 1865	North Carolina	K	40th	2087
RAWLINGS, J.J.	September 28, 1864	Virginia	I	59th	383
RAWLS, H.	May 27, 1865	North Carolina	G	3rd	2915
*RAWLS, James L.	April 5, 1865	South Carolina	A	21st	2548
RAY, A.J.	July 10, 1865	North Carolina	C	3rd - Corporal	2845
RAY, Bruce A.	March 27, 1865	North Carolina	F	53rd	2484
RAY, Charles A.	August 4, 1864	Virginia	K	22nd	7
RAY, J.W.	March 21, 1865	Tennessee	H	17th	1526
RAY, R.M.	May 18, 1865	North Carolina	E	45th	2951
RAY, S.L.	September 2, 1864	Tennessee	F	23rd	82
RAY, T.J.	January 3, 1865	Tennessee	F	23rd	1335
RAY, W.B.	November 1, 1864	Alabama	F	14th	753
RAYMOND, W.M	October 22, 1864	North Carolina	G	20th	868
RAYMOND, William M.	September 8, 1864	Virginia	H	6th Cavalry	210
RAYNER, Henry W.	January 27, 1865	North Carolina	E	8th	1653
REAMS, Nathaniel	June 10, 1865	South Carolina	A	21st	2887
REARDON, John	September 13, 1864	Virginia	C	2nd Infantry	276
REASER, Philip	July 15, 1864	Virginia	D	26th Battalion	Shohola
REAVES, Edward	September 23, 1864	North Carolina	I	11th	468
REAVES, W.L.	December 13, 1864	South Carolina	F	22nd	1124
*REDDING, Alf	August 28, 1864	North Carolina	F	2nd	48
REDDY, Andrew	May 7, 1865	Virginia	D	50th	2771

Memorial Day, looking northeast toward Davis Street.

Name	Date of Death	State	Company	Regiment/Notes	Woodlawn
REEBE, S. F.	April 13, 1865	North Carolina	G	36th	2701
REED, J.J.	August 30, 1864	South Carolina	C	4th Cavalry	95
REED, James	February 15, 1865	North Carolina	H	21st	2192
REESE, M.	September 23, 1864	Virginia	B	22nd	354
REEVES, J.W.	March 26, 1865	North Carolina	D	36th	2477
REEVES, W. H.	January 29, 1865	North Carolina	F	2nd	1798
REGAN, Jones T.	November 14, 1864	North Carolina	E	31st	807
REGAN, Neil	May 23, 1865	North Carolina	I	26th	2929
REGAN, Sugar A.	November 29, 1864	North Carolina	B	30th	1000
REID, James	March 13, 1865	South Carolina	H	25th	2436
RENALDE, E.W.	April 26, 1865	North Carolina	K	40th	1426
RENTFORD, James	March 4, 1865	North Carolina	F	10th	1988
RENTZ, G.W.	December 29, 1864	South Carolina	K	11th	1305
REULS, J. W.	July 15, 1864	North Carolina	E	31st	Shohola
REYNOLDS, B. F.	November 14, 1864	South Carolina	C	22nd	797
REYNOLDS, D.J.	May 4, 1865	Virginia	F	22nd	2758
REYNOLDS, J.W.	April 9, 1865	North Carolina	G	36th	2619
REYNOLDS, John R.	March 29, 1865	North Carolina	A	30th	2526
REYNOLDS, Jonathan N.	November 2, 1864	Virginia	E	22nd	897
REYNOLDS, William M.	March 5, 1865	North Carolina	H	35th	1971
RHODEN, W.W.	September 9, 1864	Georiga	G	16th	199
RHODES, William A.	October 29, 1864	North Carolina	E	31st	730

Name	Date of Death	State	Company	Regiment/Notes	Woodlawn
RHODES, William B.	May 24, 1865	North Carolina	A	8th	2922
RICE, Henry H.	November 16, 1864	North Carolina	B	25th	951
RICE, Thomas W.	August 27, 1864	Virginia	C	58th	99
RICH, Reuben V.	November 8, 1864	North Carolina	A	57th	830
RICHARDSON, George P.	January 11, 1865	Louisiana	F	2nd	1495
RICHARDSON, Henry E.	October 5, 1864	Virginia	C	1st – Young's Battalion	602
RICHARDSON, J.H.	November 1, 1864	Virginia	E	5th Cavalry	754
RICHARDSON, L. M.	January 27, 1865	North Carolina	B	6th	1646
RICHBOURG, R. D.	April 24, 1865	South Carolina	I	25th	1409
*RICKMAN, J.J.	September 2, 1864	North Carolina	B	18th	61
RIDDICK, E.	February 7, 1865	North Carolina	F	33rd	1921
RIDDLE, Austin	August 27, 1864	Tennessee	C	2nd Cavalry	102
RIDDLE, David C.	September 19, 1864	North Carolina	E	53rd	332
RIDGEWAY, J.	April 6, 1865	South Carolina	I	25th	2549
RIGBY, J.	May 4, 1865	Georgia	D	35th	2756
RIGGAN, J.S.	September 27, 1864	North Carolina	B	30th	387
RIGGINS, R.G.	May 2, 1865	Virginia	F	26th	2745
RIGGSBEE, Jones E.	September 15, 1864	North Carolina	D	15th	297
RIGNER, John	March 25, 1865	Tennessee	A	1st Heavy Artillery	2461
RILEY, C. P.	November 26, 1864	North Carolina	C	3rd	899
RILEY, Daniel	February 16, 1865	North Carolina	C	36th, 2nd Artillery State Troop	2203
RILEY, Joshua F.	December 6, 1864	Georgia	H	26th – Corporal	1023

Name	Date of Death	State	Company	Regiment/Notes	Woodlawn
RILEY, Judson	May 30, 1865	North Carolina	H	54th	2910
RILEY, Timothy	March 4, 1865	Virginia		Bryan's Battery	2005
RILEY, W.T.	March 6, 1865	North Carolina	C	24th - Corporal	2475
RINKE, Jacob	December 11, 1864	Alabama	D	5th	1052
RIVERS, James D.	March 16, 1865	Georgia	C	26th	1677
RIVERS, Robert L.	September 20, 1864	Georgia	I	13th	505
ROACH, Charles B.	September 29, 1864	Virginia	E	26th	440
ROAN, William L.	April 13, 1865	Virginia	E	5th Cavalry	2617
ROBERSON, Samuel	April 7, 1865	Georgia	F	61st	2656
ROBERTS, John T.	April 23, 1865	Georgia	F	38th	1399
*ROBERTS, William H.	July 25, 1864	Alabama	A	1st Battalion of Artillery	2864
ROBERTSON, Alex	September 14, 1864	North Carolina	F	37th	281
ROBERTSON, Jesse	February 19, 1865	North Carolina	F	10th	2337
ROBERTSON, N.P.	November 26, 1864	North Carolina	H	1st	980
ROBERTSON, William	March 7, 1865	North Carolina	F	10th Artillery	2407
ROBIN, John	March 7, 1865	Virginia	A	26th	2393
ROBINS, Silas	December 24, 1864	North Carolina	B	52nd	1105
ROBINS, W.W.	March 22, 1865	North Carolina	C	36th	1538
ROBINSON, Allen J.	November 8, 1864	South Carolina	I	17th	781
ROBINSON, G.H.	September 25, 1864	North Carolina	E	35th	363
ROBINSON, Harrison	March 7, 1865	North Carolina	K	10th Artillery	2405
ROBINSON, J.A.	May 4, 1865	Georgia	B	36th	2761

Name	Date of Death	State	Company	Regiment/Notes	Woodlawn
ROBINSON, J.E.	October 1, 1864	South Carolina	C	22nd	412
ROBINSON, John S.	January 29, 1865	North Carolina	C	23rd	1656
ROBINSON, Julius C.	February 15, 1865	North Carolina	I	36th, 2nd Artillery-State Troop	2170
ROBINSON, M.P.	February 18, 1865	North Carolina	H	36th	2247
ROBINSON, S.G.	September 24, 1864	Georgia	G	7th Cavalry	460
ROBINSON, William	March 10, 1865	Virginia	D	42nd	1870
ROBINSON, William H.	January 30, 1865	North Carolina	K	30th	1792
RODGERS, Charles H.	January 30, 1865	Virginia	E	4th – Miltia	1801
RODGERS, J.B.	January 28, 1865	North Carolina	E	30th	1659
RODGERS, John H.	January 22, 1865	North Carolina	D	30th	1595
RODGERS, Joseph	September 21, 1864	Virginia	K	1st Cavalry	492
RODGERS, Lewis	May 17, 1865	North Carolina	K	1st	2955
RODGERS, T.C.	February 16, 1865	South Carolina	I	21st	2188
ROGERS, A.C.	January 23, 1865	Georgia	B	7th – Corporal	1613
ROGERS, Daniel	October 11, 1864	Louisiana	C	14th	692
ROGERS, G.	February 13, 1865	Alabama	C	5th	2040
ROGERS, Henderson	March 3, 1865	Virginia	A	50th	1983
ROGERS, James C.	March 17, 1865	Alabama	C	1st Battallion of Artillery	1715
ROGERS, Sandford V.	October 31, 1864	South Carolina	C	22nd	749
ROGERS, Stephen	October 17, 1864	North Carolina	F	61st	544
ROGERS, W.J.	February 27, 1865	North Carolina	H	36th	2120
ROLLAN, A.H.	March 19, 1865	North Carolina	I	1st	1576

Name	Date of Death	State	Company	Regiment/Notes	Woodlawn
ROLLINS, O.	September 2, 1864	South Carolina	I	18th	75
*ROMINES, James	July 18, 1864	Georgia	K	21st	2851
ROOK, Permain	April 3, 1865	South Carolina	K	21st	2564
ROOK, Samuel L.	January 16, 1865	South Carolina	A	27th	1446
ROPER, William	September 7, 1864	North Carolina	B	45th	65
ROSE, James	October 16, 1864	Virginia	E	37th	562
ROSE, William H.	October 30, 1864	Virginia	C	42nd	737
ROUBLEAU, Emile	December 6, 1864	Louisiana	K	10th - Sergeant	1018
ROUSH, Henry A.	October 22, 1864	Virginia	C	38th	863
ROUSSEAUX, William	December 5, 1864	Louisiana	B	9th Battalion-Partisan Rangers	1021
ROWE, Sidney H.	December 20, 1864	North Carolina	A	12th - Corporal	1077
ROWELL, J.V.	December 20, 1864	North Carolina	H	23rd	1073
ROWLAND, C. H.	October 2, 1864	North Carolina	C	8th	627
ROYAL, Noah	February 2, 1865	Georgia	E	Cobb's Legion	1767
ROYAL, W.M.	March 15, 1865	North Carolina	A	37th	1569
ROYALS, William B.	November 28, 1864	Georgia	H	64th	988
ROZIER, Evander C.	November 23, 1864	North Carolina	D	51st	922
RUDISIL, W.V.	May 28, 1865	South Carolina	D	17th	2911
RUDISILL, G.A.	August 19, 1864	South Carolina	H	6th - Corporal	119
RUNKLE, Charles	September 16, 1864	Virginia	F	2nd - Corproal	307
RUNRAGE, William	October 3, 1864	North Carolina	F	5th	617
RUPPE, W. W.	September 9, 1864	South Carolina	K	Holcombe Legion - Corporal	204

Name	Date of Death	State	Company	Regiment/Notes	Woodlawn
RUSS, William	April 8, 1865	North Carolina	C	8th –Corporal	2622
RUSSELL, D. D.	December 25, 1864	North Carolina	H	21st	1108
RUSSELL, J. B.	September 13, 1864	South Carolina	A	1st Rifles	267
RUSSELL, Joel	February 4, 1865	North Carolina	B	5th	1744
RUSSELL, John	March 4, 1864	North Carolina	G	40th, 3rd Artillery-State Troop	1975
RUSTIN, B. W.	August 19, 1864	Georgia	H	7th Cavalry	120
RUTHERFORD, John	March 25, 1865	Georgia	I	35th	2459
RYALS, Joseph	September 17, 1864	North Carolina	I	61st	315
RYAN, J. C.	September 17, 1864	North Carolina	M	16th	317
RYKARD, J. H.	September 5, 1864	South Carolina	C	6th Cavalry	243
RYLANDER, Joel F.	April 9, 1865	Alabama	A	1st Battalion of Artillery	2604
SADDLER, Green	December 28, 1864	Alabama	E	14th	1303
*SADLER, William	January 19, 1865	South Carolina	E	20th Volunteer Infantry	1205
SAMKINS, T. C.	July 15, 1864	Georgia	C	2nd Cavalry	Shohola
SANDERS, B. T.	March 1, 1865	Georgia	C	16th	2108
SANDERS, Stephen	September 14, 1864	North Carolina	C	42nd	294
SANDERSON, Samuel	January 19, 1865	Alabama	E	1st Battalion of Artillery	1196
SANFORD, J.	March 20, 1865	South Carolina	G	25th	1549
SANFORD, J.F.	July 15, 1864	North Carolina	A	44th	Shohola
SANFORD, William P.	February 14, 1865	Alabama	E	61st	2035
SANGFORD, W. B.	July 15, 1864	Georgia	K	16th	Shohola
SAPP, Lemuel	December 22, 1864	Georgia	I	21st	1088

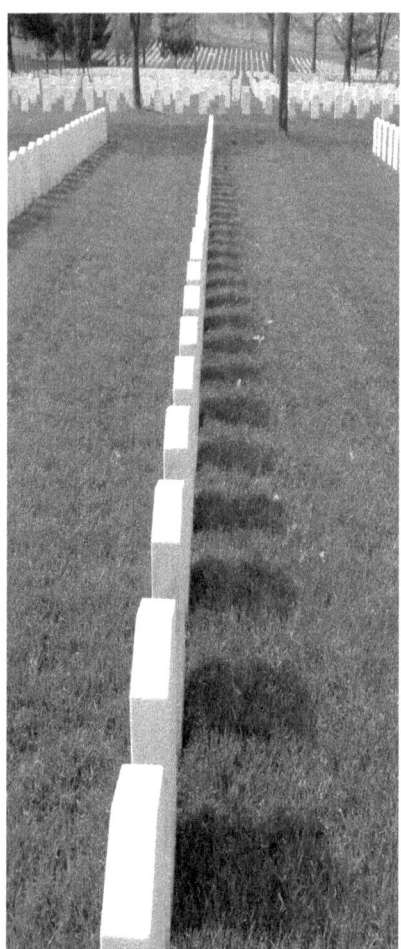

The Confederate portion of Woodlawn National Cemetery is about two acres in size.

Brothers William and Isaac Saddler/Sadler were captured in late July 1864 at the First Battle of Deep Bottom. They were initially remanded to Point Lookout, Maryland but were subsequently transferred to Elmira on August 8, 1864. William died January 19, 1865, his cause of death cited as chronic diarrhea. Isaac was paroled for exchange on February 20, 1865 and transferred to Point Lookout.

I am, of course, anxious that William Saddler be listed with his unit - the 20th South Carolina Volunteer Infantry, Company E, under the command of Captain James Addison Cowan of Kershaw's brigade. They were from Anderson, South Carolina.

My great-grandfather served with the Saddlers. He was not captured at Deep Bottom but was wounded in October 1864 while detached to General Jubal Early in the Shenandoah Valley.

I have been researching his unit as I was impressed by this "band of brothers" who all grew up together in one small community in Anderson County, South Carolina. There were fathers and sons, brothers, cousins, and in-laws all within this one unit. Their families back home worked, worshipped, and struggled together while awaiting the unit's return.

To my knowledge, these two brothers were the only ones imprisoned at Elmira. Sadly, while transferred for exchange Isaac Saddler apparently did not return home either and died at Point Lookout. He left two children and a widow.

Submitted by James R. Shaw.

Name	Date of Death	State	Company	Regiment/Notes	Woodlawn
SAPT, F. W.	July 15, 1864	North Carolina	E	22nd	Shohola
SARTIN, A. H.	July 13, 1865	Tennessee	K	44th - Sergeant	2869
SATTERFIELD, Jacob	January 5, 1865	North Carolina	G	37th	1244
SATTERFIELD, L. H.	June 24, 1865	North Carolina	F	8th - Sergeant	2821
SATTERWHITE, John	March 19, 1865	Alabama	A	21st	1582
SATTERWHITE, Philip	April 5, 1865	Alabama	A	21st	2546
SAUNDERS, Aaron	February 3, 1865	North Carolina	H	45th	1755
SAUNDERS, E.M.	May 5, 1865	North Carolina	I	5th	2763
SAUNDERS, T. C.	February 16, 1865	South Carolina	C	15th Cavalry	2200
SAUNDERS, Vincent M.	October 8, 1864	Virginia	K	50th	654
SAUNDERS, W. R.	January 29, 1865	Virginia	D	44th	2828
SAVAGE, Wesley	September 14, 1864	North Carolina	D	24th	280
SAWYER, Charles	March 15, 1865	North Carolina	A	32nd - Corporal	1667
SAWYER, Edwin	December 16, 1864	Virginia	B	6th	1272
SAWYER, John	March 26, 1865	North Carolina	I	32nd	2469
SAWYER, Simeon T.	January 5, 1865	North Carolina	A	32nd - Sergeant	1255
SCHOCKLEY, William D.	September 14, 1864	Alabama	B	Love's Batalion - Cavalry	291
SCHOLLS, T.	March 7, 1865	Virginia	I	26th	2389
SCHULL, Anthony	October 7, 1864	North Carolina	I	11th	651
SCOGGINS, A. J.	June 22, 1865	North Carolina	I	45th - Corporal	2814
SCOGGINS, J.L.	March 9, 1865	Texas		23rd Cavalry	2360
SCOGGINS, John M.	December 26, 1864	Georgia	C	64th	1285

Name	Date of Death	State	Company	Regiment/Notes	Woodlawn
SCOTT, Henry W.	February 13, 1865	North Carolina	I	21st	2070
SCOTT, John D.	September 12, 1864	Georgia	B	35th	175
SCOTT, T.M.	December 21, 1864	North Carolina	I	21st	1082
SCOTT, William H.	January 23, 1865	North Carolina	D	5th	1600
SEAY, Daniel	January 30, 1865	South Carolina	E	7th Cavalry	1786
SECRIST, Daniel	March 17, 1865	Virginia	I	10th - Corporal	1714
SECRIST, L. A.	April 13, 1865	North Carolina	K	10th	2717
SEEBERT, Lanty L.	November 11, 1864	Virginia	I	25th - Corporal	825
SEECHRIST, James	May 10, 1865	North Carolina	I	14th	2790
SEGARS, Wiley	February 5, 1865	Georgia	D	12th	1907
SEIVERS, William	November 24, 1864	Louisiana	F	15th	915
SELL, Andrew	February 16, 1865	South Carolina	K	21st	2187
SELLARS, William	February 10, 1865	North Carolina	D	36th, 2nd Artillery-State Troop	1944
SELLERS, David	March 20, 1865	North Carolina	E	36th	1544
SELLERS, G.	May 21, 1865	North Carolina	D	36th	2916
SELLERS, John	March 1, 1865	North Carolina	F	36th	2023
SELLERS, John	April 5, 1865	North Carolina	G	36th, 2nd Artillery - Sergeant	2537
SELLERS, John M.	March 20, 1865	North Carolina	G	36th, 2nd Artillery - State Troop	1560
SELLERS, John W.	May 14, 1865	North Carolina	G	36th, 2nd Artillery	2804
*SELLERS, W. R.	March 23, 1865	South Carolina	A	4th Cavalry	2438
SELRODER, S.	March 4, 1865	South Carolina	G	27th	1978
SENTER, John W.	January 3, 1865	Virginia	D	36th	1506

Name	Date of Death	State	Company	Regiment/Notes	Woodlawn
SESSOMS, P.T.	October 12, 1864	North Carolina	H	55th	573
SEWARD, R.	August 11, 1864	Virginia	G	26th	131
SEXTON, Alex	February 19, 1865	North Carolina	C	31st	2330
SEXTON, Joseph	January 15, 1865	North Carolina	A	37th	1444
SHADLING, J. N.	March 31, 1865	North Carolina	H	36th	2598
SHAFFNER, G.W.	March 15, 1865	Virginia	F	53rd	1683
SHANNON, John A.	April 6, 1865	Alabama	C	61st	2630
SHARING, J. D.	October 4, 1864	North Carolina	B	30th	639
SHARP, P. B.	October 10, 1864	North Carolina	E	31st	676
SHAW, Alex E.	May 8, 1865	Georgia	E	3rd	2777
SHAW, Archibald	March 24, 1865	North Carolina	D	50th	2449
SHAW, F. E.	March 6, 1865	North Carolina	E	32nd - Sergeant	2415
SHEA, John	December 1, 1864	Louisiana	B	15th	1014
SHEARER, B. H.	August 11, 1864	South Carolina	G	7th Cavalry	14
SHEARIN, H. L. W.	October 21, 1864	Tennessee	G	44th	873
SHEETS, W. L.	February 12, 1865	Virginia	K	2nd	2076
SHEETZ, Samuel	March 1, 1865	Virginia	G	2nd	2101
SHEFFEY, William B.	September 2, 1864	Virginia	D	4th	64
SHEFLER, B. F.	March 26, 1865	Virginia	D	46th	2480
SHEFLET, B. F.	June 30, 1865	Virginia	D	46th	2824
SHEFLETT, M.	February 27, 1865	Virginia	D	46th	2156
SHELBY, W.J.	October 31, 1864	Alabama	F	1st Battalion of Artillery	741

Name	Date of Death	State	Company	Regiment/Notes	Woodlawn
SHELFER, E. K.	September 30, 1864	North Carolina	E	3rd Cavalry	402
SHELLER, John	January 28, 1865	Virginia	K	50th - Sergeant	1810
SHELTON, Alf	September 25, 1864	North Carolina	B	6th	372
SHELTON, E. B.	September 21, 1864	Virginia	A	40th -Sergeant	347
SHELTON, William H.	January 27, 1865	Virginia	H	42nd	1645
SHEPPARD, D.	September 18, 1864	North Carolina	B	1st	151
SHEPPARD, George W.	November 19, 1864	Alabama	I	5th	946
SHERIFF, Thomas M.	February 25, 1865	Georgia	H	24th	2291
SHERISH, W. L.	February 16, 1865	South Carolina	C	4th Cavalry	2198
SHERLOR, J.	February 16, 1865	Virginia	K	50th	2181
SHERMAN, John	October 3, 1864	Virginia	B	18th Cavalry	637
SHERRILL, N.	March 29, 1865	North Carolina	F	32nd	2538
SHERRILL, William P.	January 27, 1865	North Carolina	F	32nd	1644
SHINARD, John	April 6, 1865	Virginia	I	14th	2628
SHIPES, Jacob	December 8, 1864	South Carolina	D	11th	1174
SHIPP, William L.	September 26, 1864	Georgia	G	31st	370
SHIRER, Henry	June 30, 1865	South Carolina	F	25th	2830
SHIVER, W. N. W.	December 1, 1864	Florida	A	1st Reserve	1004
SHOCKLEY, W.S.	February 5, 1865	Georgia	C	18th	1902
SHOE, Constine	September 18, 1864	North Carolina	F	37th	513
SHOOK, Henry	August 16, 1864	North Carolina	A	18th	24
SHORE, Sanford	April 18, 1865	North Carolina	F	32nd	1359

Name	Date of Death	State	Company	Regiment/Notes	Woodlawn
SHUMATE, Daniel	January 6, 1865	North Carolina	F	52nd	1235
SHUTTLESWORTH, H.	April 9, 1865	Alabama	C	1st Battalion of Artillery	2623
SHYTLE, A. S.	June 19, 1865	North Carolina	D	1st	2809
SICHRIST, Charles	October 6, 1864	Virginia	B	2nd	595
SIDES, C. D.	February 8, 1865	North Carolina	I	5th	1956
SIGMAN, Martin M.	November 14, 1864	North Carolina	C	28th	809
SILLS, Levi	December 10, 1864	North Carolina	A	2nd	1035
SIMMONDS, Calvin	March 25, 1865	North Carolina	C	25th	2452
SIMMONS, E.J.	October 2, 1864	North Carolina	A	2nd	634
SIMMONS, Elvin	February 17, 1865	Alabama	F	1st Battalion of Artillery	2207
*SIMMONS, H.	April 10, 1865	North Carolina	C	28th	2672
*SIMMONS, J. F.	March 13, 1865	North Carolina	A	2nd	1834
SIMMONS, J. H.	February 24, 1865	North Carolina	C	36th	2269
SIMMONS, Jesse	March 22, 1865	North Carolina	D	20th	1540
SIMMONS, Joseph	February 18, 1865	Virginia	B	Hood's Battalion	2222
SIMMONS, Joshua M.	March 3, 1865	North Carolina	A	18th	1989
SIMMONS, Malcolm L.	November 23, 1864	North Carolina	I	51st	990
SIMMONS, Moses	September 14, 1864	North Carolina	G	20th	275
SIMMONS, Peter	September 29, 1864	North Carolina	A	2nd	426
SIMPSON, John F.	January 19, 1865	South Carolina	F	Holcombe Legion	1429
SIMPSON, W. A.	December 5, 1864	South Carolina	G	3rd	1029
SIMS, Miles	March 19, 1865	Florida	C	1st Reserve	1571

Name	Date of Death	State	Company	Regiment/Notes	Woodlawn
SINGLETERRY, C.	February 24, 1865	North Carolina	K	40th	2287
SINGLETERRY, J.T.	March 6, 1865	North Carolina	K	18th	2390
SINGLETON, F. M.	January 29, 1865	Georgia	E	24th	1806
SINGLETON, George F.	March 30, 1865	Louisiana	H	6th-Hospital Steward	2533
SINGLETON, Obediah	December 26, 1864	Virginia	F	2nd - Corporal	1107
SINGLETON, Samuel	February 28, 1865	Georgia	H	4th	2114
SIPE, Jacob	January 5, 1865	Virginia	E	10th - Corporal	1249
SIZEMORE, Aaron	March 1, 1865	Alabama	C	1st Battalion of Artillery	2104
SIZEMORE, Edward	November 19, 1864	South Carolina	C	22nd	948
SIZEMORE, William J.	March 21, 1865	North Carolina	B	40th, 3rd Artillery	1528
SKINNER, Benjamin F.	September 23, 1864	North Carolina	A	1st	470
SKINNER, Franklin	April 9, 1865	South Carolina	H	21st	2612
SKINNER, J.J.	January 1, 1865	Georgia	I	16th	1342
SLADE, William F.	January 1, 1865	Alabama	A	21st	1332
SLADER, Henry C.	February 1, 1865	North Carolina	I	5th	1764
SLATON, John A.	November 27, 1864	Virginia	F	58th	896
SMALL, A. C.	December 7, 1864	South Carolina	K	26th	1185
SMATHERS, William J.	November 2, 1864	North Carolina	C	Thomas Legion - Sergeant	762
SMATLEY, G.C.	July 15, 1864	Georgia	C	Legion	Shohola
SMITH, A.G.	August 31, 1864	North Carolina	F	43rd	91
SMITH, A.J.	September 5, 1864	South Carolina	F	Holcombe Legion	239
SMITH, B. F.	May 3, 1865	South Carolina	E	11th	2753

Name	Date of Death	State	Company	Regiment/Notes	Woodlawn
SMITH, Bracey	September 20, 1864	North Carolina	G	51st	194
SMITH, Chesley	June 23, 1865	North Carolina	A	36th, 2nd Artillery	2817
SMITH, Coleman	September 4, 1864	Tennessee	B	1st	227
SMITH, D.	March 29, 1865	North Carolina	K	40th	2517
SMITH, E.H.	February 8, 1865	Georgia	C,	4th	1924
SMITH, E. P.	February 20, 1865	South Carolina	E	6th Cavalry	2322
SMITH, Edwin	February 8, 1865	North Carolina	I	36th	2352
SMITH, Elias	February 8, 1865	North Carolina	H	36th	1931
SMITH, Evan	April 2, 1865	North Carolina	K	28th	2579
*SMITH, Fred	March 4, 1865	North Carolina	D	14th Heavy Artillery	2105
SMITH, Freeman	February 22, 1865	North Carolina	A	28th	2303
SMITH, General M.	January 31, 1865	Georgia	D	26th	1782
SMITH, George	October 25, 1864	North Carolina	G	28th	855
SMITH, George	February 4, 1865	Tennessee	F	63rd	1897
SMITH, Herbert M.	September 16, 1864	South Carolina	E	4th Cavalry	304
SMITH, Isaac	November 2, 1864	Alabama	H	44th	843
SMITH, Isaac	September 17, 1864	Alabama	H	6th	160
SMITH, J.C.	May 11, 1865	Georgia	D	21st -Corporal	2796
SMITH, J.H.	October 27, 1864	Georgia	B	7th Cavalry	721
SMITH, J.J.	March 2, 1865	Georgia	B	16th	2103
SMITH, J.W.	March 7, 1865	Alabama	A	1st Battalion of Artillery	2403
SMITH, J.W.	February 8, 1865	South Carolina	F	Holcombe Legion	1932

Name	Date of Death	State	Company	Regiment/Notes	Woodlawn
SMITH, J.W.	January 9, 1865	South Carolina	C	17th	1216
SMITH, James	December 27, 1864	Louisiana	A	Ogden's Battalion	1298
SMITH, James F.	March 16, 1865	South Carolina	I	25th Cavalry	1554
SMITH, James H.	January 9, 1865	Tennessee	C	63rd	1217
SMITH, Jesse S.	February 1, 1865	Georgia	K	9th	1763
SMITH, John B.	February 8, 1865	North Carolina	G	40th, 3rd Artillery - State Troop 1936	
SMITH, John D.	March 22, 1865	North Carolina	I	36th, 2nd Artillery	1523
SMITH, John H.	February 14, 1865	Virginia	C	51st	2027
SMITH, John H.	September 27, 1864	North Carolina	B	45th	389
SMITH, John N.	April 9, 1865	North Carolina	K	28th	2627
SMITH, John O.	December 19, 1864	Virginia	I	50th	1072
SMITH, John P.	April 10, 1865	North Carolina	I	36th	2609
SMITH, John W.	November 10, 1864	Virginia	G	42nd	939
SMITH, Nathan	February 24, 1865	North Carolina	A	36th, 2nd Artillery	2267
SMITH, Noah	February 26, 1865	Virginia	E	42nd	2280
SMITH, Norman	March 12, 1865	North Carolina	A	1st	2006
SMITH, Osceola	December 12, 1864	Virginia	H	40th	1147
SMITH, Peter W.	March 13, 1865	North Carolina	H	36th, 2nd Artillery	2432
SMITH, R.J.	February 27, 1865	South Carolina	F	25th	2159
SMITH, R. M.	November 16, 1864	South Carolina	B	4th Cavalry	954
SMITH, S. H.	March 1, 1865	North Carolina	D	36th	2098

Name	Date of Death	State	Company	Regiment/Notes	Woodlawn
SMITH, S. N.	October 27, 1864	North Carolina	D	8th	716
SMITH, Samuel A.	September 24, 1864	Louisiana	F	2nd	366
*SMITH, T. John	February 17, 1865	Alabama	A	1st Battalion of Artillery	2226
SMITH, Thomas	February 8, 1865	Virginia	B	30th Battalion	1935
SMITH, Thomas	October 13, 1864	Virginia	B	42nd - Corporal	703
SMITH, W.M.	April 11, 1865	Georgia	C	24th	2683
SMITH, W.T.	February 26, 1865	Alabama	H	10th	2294
SMITH, William	January 31, 1865	Virginia	H	22nd Cavalry	1779
SMOKE, H.E.	February 21, 1865	South Carolina	H	25th	2264
SMYRE, L.	March 6, 1865	North Carolina	K	46th	1963
SNEAD, James N.	February 22, 1865	Georgia	E	3rd Battalion-Sharpshooters	2236
SNELL, Swain S.	April 4, 1865	North Carolina	G	1st	2566
SNEPES, John	February 20, 1865	North Carolina	G	40th	2326
SNODDY, J.	October 28, 1864	South Carolina	C	25th	727
SNOW, Delaware	September 19, 1864	Virginia	D	46th	516
SNYDER, J.H.	January 19, 1865	North Carolina		Citizen of North Carolina	1197
SOLES, A.	April 8, 1865	Virginia	C	44th	2644
SOLES, H.I.	December 31, 1864	North Carolina	C	18th	1322
SOOTS, Adam	March 1, 1865	North Carolina	C	3rd Battalion-Artillery	2097
SOUTH, E.C.	February 15, 1865	Tennessee	K	63rd	2191
SOUTHARD, Levi	April 6, 1865	North Carolina	A	28th	2638
SOUTHERS, James	November 14, 1864	Virginia	C	51st	800

Name	Date of Death	State	Company	Regiment/Notes	Woodlawn
*SPARKMAN, W. P.	October 13, 1864	North Carolina	F	51st	701
SPARKS, Charles B.	January 1, 1865	Louisiana	I	2nd Cavalry	1327
SPARKS, Hugh	September 11, 1864	North Carolina	C	13th	249
SPARKS, Welcome U.	November 10, 1864	Georgia	B	35th	787
SPEAR, William	May 3, 1865	North Carolina	G	18th	2907
SPELL, David	March 24, 1865	North Carolina	C	36th	2456
SPELL, Hardy	February 13, 1865	North Carolina	C	36th	2044
SPENCER, J.J.	April 20, 1865	Virginia	H	28th	1382
SPENCER, Jasper	November 28, 1864	South Carolina	G	18th	991
SPENCER, John	February 10, 1865	North Carolina	D	36th	2086
SPIVRY, William	January 23, 1865	North Carolina	H	33rd	1593
SPOTTS, Jacob	December 28, 1864	Virginia	F	1st Cavalry	1300
SPRING, W.	February 19, 1865	South Carolina	A	21st	2340
SPRING, William	March 11, 1865	Georgia	D	64th	2428
SPRINGS, Aaron	March 11, 1865	North Carolina	H	3rd	1841
SPRINKLE, M.	October 4, 1864	North Carolina	I	18th	607
SPROUSE, Jacob M.	December 30, 1864	Virginia	L	31st	1310
STACEY, N. R.	March 7, 1865	South Carolina	K	18th	2386
STACKHOUSE, John W.	September 10, 1864	South Carolina	E	4th	520
STALLINGS, Octavius	November 26, 1864	North Carolina	C	12th	981
STALLINGS, Slade R.	March 10, 1865	North Carolina	K	10th, 1st Artillery-State Troop	1884

> Mr Marshel Talor Death
> he Dide in Prison Camp at Elmira
> State N y on the 28 Day of August
> in the yeare of 1864 Priviet Co A
> 37 North Corlinia Regyment NC

Marshall Taylor was the youngest son in the family to join the army. He enlisted March 11, 1864 at Liberty Mills, Virginia. He enlisted into the 37th North Carolina Infantry, Company A with the promise of $12-per month pay - which was never received. His regiment fought in the Battle of the Wilderness and at the Spotsylvania courthouse. Captured in Spotsylvania with 4,000 other prisoners, he was sent to Belle Plain, Virginia, then Point Lookout, Maryland (arrived May 7), then to Elmira (arrived August 8). He died in Elmira on August 29 of pneumonia. See more on page 18.

Above is the death notice that was sent to his family.

Submitted by Wayne Taylor.

Name	Date of Death	State	Company	Regiment/Notes	Woodlawn
STALLINGS, William C.	January 29, 1865	Georgia	B	45th	1807
STALNECKED, B. F.	October 7, 1864	North Carolina	H	7th	585
STARLING, D.J.	April 12, 1865	North Carolina	G	33rd	2686
STARNES, David A.	October 18, 1864	North Carolina	A	18th	678
STRANES, E.	January 12, 1865	North Carolina	H	30th	1488
STATE, Frederick	September 17, 1864	Louisiana	C, D	14th	164
STAUFFER, Napoleon B.	July 15, 1864	North Carolina	D	42nd	Shohola
STEADMAN, William	January 19, 1865	North Carolina	K	37th	1200
STEAN, Allen	February 17, 1865	South Carolina	F	21st	2221
STENSON, Joseph C.	December 11, 1864	Alabama	C	1st - Artillery - Corporal	1091
STEPHENS, J.A.	January 3, 1865	Georgia	E	53rd	1346
STEPHENS, James E.	March 14, 1865	Georgia	G	3rd Battallion-Sharpshooters	2434
STEPHENS, Jesse	February 15, 1865	Tennessee	E	1st Artillery	2179
STEPHENS, Perry	February 19, 1865	South Carolina	G	27th	2341
STEPHENSON, Bennett	March 19, 1865	North Carolina	G	5th	1563
STEPHENSON, J.C.	August 27, 1864	North Carolina	G	37th	103
STEPHENSON, J. E.	February 28, 1865	South Carolina	Holcombe Legion		2138
STEPP, Silas H.	January 2, 1865	North Carolina	C	6th Cavalry	1340
STERLING, G.P.	March 11, 1865	South Carolina	B	3rd	1836
STEVENS, E.	February 23, 1865	South Carolina	I	21st	2254
STEVENS, J. E.	October 10, 1864	North Carolina	C	18th	682
STEWART, A.	March 14, 1865	North Carolina	D	36th	1668

Name	Date of Death	State	Company	Regiment/Notes	Woodlawn
STEWART, Charles A.	March 14, 1865	North Carolina	A - State Troop	36th, 2nd Artillery - Musician	1669
STEWART, Elijah	November 11, 1864	Virginia	G	45th	824
STEWART, J.	April 9, 1865	North Carolina	D	36th	2610
STEWART, J.J.	February 17, 1865	Alabama		Jeff Davis Artillery	2224
STEWART, J. Martin	March 21, 1865	North Carolina	H	56th	1547
STEWART, J.W.	April 24, 1865	South Carolina	B	25th	1410
STEWART, James	October 5, 1864	North Carolina	C	35th	641
STEWART, Samuel	April 4, 1865	South Carolina	B	21st	2555
STEWART, W.D.	September 16, 1864	Georgia	A	38th	173
STEWART, William B.	November 5, 1864	Georgia	D	64th	766
STILL, James T.	January 6, 1865	South Carolina	H	17th	1234
STILLWELL, William	November 16, 1864	Virginia	I	22nd Cavalry	959
STINSON, Elias D.	January 2, 1865	Alabama	C	1st Battalion of Artillery	1341
STINSON, H.M.	May 17, 1865	North Carolina	I	31st	2956
STINSON, John W.	March 23, 1865	Alabama	A	1st Battalion of Artillery	1511
*STINSON, L.	February 11, 1865	Alabama	A	1st Battalion of Artillery	2058
STOCKDALE, Henry T.	August 18, 1864	Virginia	G	52nd	118
*STOCKDALE, William J.	July 9, 1864	Virginia	G	52nd	2854
STOKES, W.J.	March 12, 1865	Tennessee	B	1st Heavy Artillery	1822
STOLLINGS, J.W.	April 17, 1865	North Carolina	F	45th	1351
STONE, William	September 10, 1864	North Carolina	I	13th	255
STONECYPHER, John H.	September 25, 1864	Georgia	H	42nd - Corporal	365

Name	Date of Death	State	Company	Regiment/Notes	Woodlawn
STORGEAL, J.	January 22, 1865	North Carolina	K	23rd	1578
STORY, B. F.	August 25, 1864	Georgia	A	7th Cavalry	43
STRAWBRIDGE, W.J.	September 6, 1864	Alabama	C	41st	245
STRICKLAND, A.	April 23, 1865	North Carolina	E	36th	1402
STRICKLAND, Alex	February 18, 1865	North Carolina	E	36th, 2nd Artillery	2216
STRICKLAND, Jacob	May 16, 1865	North Carolina	E	30th	2959
STRICKLAND, Maston	April 8, 1865	North Carolina	A	36th	2602
STRICKLAND, N.	March 12, 1865	North Carolina	E	36th	1848
STRICKLAND, Samuel	August 4, 1864	North Carolina	H	31st	6
STRICKLAND, Thomas J.	July 15, 1864	North Carolina	I	51st	Shohola
STRIDER, James M. A.	October 13, 1864	North Carolina	H	3rd	565
STRIDER, Joel	September 20, 1864	North Carolina	B	52nd	507
STROMAN, C.	May 10, 1865	South Carolina	F	25th	2788
STRONG, Andrew	October 30, 1864	South Carolina	D	17th	732
STROUP, A.	December 9, 1864	South Carolina	K	18th	1167
STUART, Michael K.	May 1, 1865	Georgia	H	12th	2741
STUBBS, S. F.	February 11, 1865	South Carolina	F	21st	2059
STUKES, Alfred	September 2, 1864	South Carolina	D	4th Cavalry	87
STULTZ, Lafayette A.	October 16, 1864	Virginia	F	24th	555
STUMP, George T.	February 4, 1865	Virginia	B	42nd	1888
*STURGEON, H.	April 5, 1865	Mississippi	E	10th Battalion	2558
STURGEON, R. D.	December 10, 1864	South Carolina	H	7th Battalion	1055

Name	Date of Death	State	Company	Regiment/Notes	Woodlawn
STURM, W. G.	October 10, 1864	Tennessee	F	63rd - Corporal	677
SUGGS, James McR.	April 19, 1865	North Carolina	H	36th, 2nd Artillery-State Troop	1371
SULLENS, Andrew	February 22, 1865	Virginia	B	48th	2249
SULLIVAN, Hardy	April 20, 1865	North Carolina	F	10th	1383
SULLIVAN, Richard T.	February 28, 1865	North Carolina	I	36th	2144
SULLIVAN, W. J.	March 4, 1865	South Carolina	B	29th	1979
SUMMERLAND, Wiley	March 20, 1865	North Carolina	F	10th Artillery	1545
SUMMERS, James B.	April 4, 1865	Alabama	I	5th	2563
SUMMERS, John	October 12, 1864	Virginia	A	25th	564
SUMMIT, H. P.	November 16, 1864	North Carolina	H	28th	960
*SUMNERS, Matthew	December 6, 1864	Georgia	D	64th	1017
SURRENCY, Wiley	March 30, 1865	Georgia	G	20th Battalion Cavalry	2529
SUTER, W. F.	October 13, 1864	North Carolina	C	33rd	705
SUTTON, Bryan	March 6, 1865	North Carolina	F	10th, 1st Artillery	2414
SUTTON, John B.	September 23, 1864	North Carolina	A	18th	355
SUTTON, John C.	April 16, 1865	North Carolina	G	36th, 2nd Artillery	2716
SUTTON, R. M.	May 9, 1865	Florida	K	10th	2783
SUTTON, Sanford	January 4, 1865	North Carolina	I	8th - Sergeant	1256
SWADLEY, J.	November 3, 1864	Virginia	I	25tht - Sergeant	761
SWAIN, William	January 9, 1865	North Carolina	D	8th	1219
SWANN, S. D.	February 21, 1865	North Carolina	G	44th	2304
SWINT, Andrew J.	March 4, 1865	Georgia	F	21st	1965

OATH OF ALLEGIANCE

"I, --------, do solemnly swear, in presence of Almighty God, that I will henceforth faithfully support, protect and defend the Constitution of the United States, and the union of the States thereunder; and that I will, in like manner, abide by and faithfully support all acts of Congress passed during the existing rebellion with reference to slaves, so long and so far as not repealed, modified or held void by Congress, or by decision of the Supreme Court; and that I will, in like manner, abide by and faithfully support all proclamations of the President made during the existing rebellion having reference to slaves, so long and so far as not modified or declared void by decision of the Supreme Court. So help me God."

During the time of the Elmira Prison Camp, prisoners of war were often released upon taking an "oath of allegiance." Prisoners who swore to this were called "Oathies." This is an excerpt from Abraham Lincoln's *Proclamation of Amnesty and Reconstruction* dated December 8, 1863. Actual wording varied between locales.

Name	Date of Death	State	Company	Regiment/Notes	Woodlawn
SWINT, John	January 18, 1865	Virginia	F	21st	1441
SYDENSTRICKER, J.H.	February 6, 1865	Virginia	D	26th Battalion - Corporal	1906
SYKES, Amos	May 6, 1865	North Carolina	I	36th	2766
SYKES, Edmund	March 3, 1865	North Carolina	C	36th	1991
SYLVESTER, Gordon	March 8, 1865	North Carolina	D	13th	2408
TABLER, Jesse	May 3, 1865	North Carolina	K	12th	2752
TACKETT, J.C.	April 25, 1865	North Carolina	H	5th	2726
TALLAH, J.J.	September 12, 1864	North Carolina	H	22nd	187
TALLAVAST, Alex	April 4, 1865	South Carolina	B	20th	2556
TALLEY, H.	February 3, 1865	Tennessee	H	25th	1746
TALLEY, Timothy A.	December 10, 1864	Alabama	E	1st Artillery	1043
TALLEY, W. Goode	February 4, 1865	Virginia	K	12th	1899
TANKERSLY, John	March 24, 1865	Alabama	F	6th	2462
TARPLEY, R.	January 13, 1865	Tennessee	K	7th	1475
TATUM, A.J.	March 13, 1865	North Carolina	H	36th	1832
TATUM, Silas E.	May 20, 1865	Georgia	H	38th	2941
TAYLOR, A.	February 15, 1865	Alabama	E	61st	2190
TAYLOR, A.J.	August 30, 1864	Tennessee	A	1st - Corporal	92
TAYLOR, Blount	July 4, 1865	North Carolina	A	3rd - Sergeant	2835
TAYLOR, Cary	December 27, 1864	Florida		Jones Company-1st Reserve	1301
TAYLOR, Charles S.	March 4, 1865	Virginia	F	56th	1985
*TAYLOR, David B.	March 4, 1865	North Carolina	F	57th	2004

Name	Date of Death	State	Company	Regiment/Notes	Woodlawn
TAYLOR, David C.	December 4, 1864	North Carolina	K	8th	879
TAYLOR, E.E.	September 12, 1864	Virginia	E	6th	193
TAYLOR, J.J.	March 11, 1865	North Carolina	A	36th	1861
*TAYLOR, J.J.	September 29, 1864	North Carolina	E	7th – Sergeant	429
TAYLOR, Jacob	October 1, 1864	North Carolina	H	5th	411
TAYLOR, James T.	February 16, 1865	North Carolina	K	40th	2208
TAYLOR, John	March 24, 1865	North Carolina	H	1st – Sergeant	2446
TAYLOR, Joy S.	December 25, 1864	North Carolina	E	41st – Sergeant	1111
TAYLOR, Marshall	August 29, 1864	North Carolina	A	37th	52
TAYLOR, S.P.	August 20, 1864	Alabama	D	8th	115
TAYLOR, Samuel W.	November 12, 1864	Georgia	K	64th	820
TAYLOR, W.C.	February 26, 1865	Texas	H	34th Cavalry	2295
TAYLOR, William	June 2, 1865	North Carolina	G	8th	2902
TAYLOR, William W.	March 10, 1865	Alabama	A	21st	1858
TEACHEY, William	August 15, 1864	North Carolina	G	51st	23
TEAFORD, John H.	September 21, 1864	Virginia	H	25th	362
*TEAGUE, O.S.	November 21, 1864	Alabama		Jeff Davis Artillery	933
TEAGUE, U.S.	April 25, 1865	North Carolina	E	37th	1420
TEAGUE, W.C.	February 1, 1865	South Carolina	E	6th Cavalry	1769
TEEL, G.W.	April 7, 1865	South Carolina	D	21st	2646
TERRY, Horton	November 13, 1864	Alabama	E	1st Battalion of Artillery	815
TERRY, Thomas D.	February 14, 1865	Alabama	G	6th	2061

Name	Date of Death	State	Company	Regiment/Notes	Woodlawn
TEW, Alex	November 2, 1864	North Carolina	I	51st	845
TEW, Jackson	October 22, 1864	North Carolina	I	51st	722
TEW, James W.	December 2, 1864	North Carolina	I	51st	891
THIGPEN, B.	April 19, 1865	North Carolina	B	3rd	1366
THIVEATT, S.N.	October 21, 1864	Tennessee	I	44th	871
THOMAS, J.C.	December 7, 1864	Florida	I	5th Battalion - Cavalry	1180
THOMAS, J.H.	March 6, 1865	North Carolina	C	18th	2419
THOMAS, James	March 8, 1865	North Carolina	A	1st	2369
THOMAS, John A.	February 17, 1865	Arkansas	G	3rd	2228
THOMAS, Philip	October 1, 1864	South Carolina	E	5th Cavalry	421
THOMAS, R.H.	June 13, 1865	Virginia	G	34th	2882
THOMAS, Robert H. B.	October 16, 1864	North Carolina	D	30th - Corporal	561
THOMAS, Silas	November 25, 1864	North Carolina	K	47th - Corporal	912
THOMAS, W.	March 17, 1865	South Carolina	F	13th	1717
THOMAS, William N.	February 4, 1865	Georgia	G	21st	1889
THOMASON, John B.	February 12, 1865	Virginia	D	34th	2028
THOMPSON, Andrew J.	January 16, 1865	Alabama	E	1st Battalion of Artillery	1445
THOMPSON, Francis M.	October 25, 1864	Alabama	R	1st Battalion of Artillery	848
THOMPSON, H.	October 21, 1864	South Carolina	G	23rd	870
THOMPSON, H.	November 26, 1864	Alabama	G	12th	905
*THOMPSON, J.A.	October 7, 1864	Alabama	G	12th	587
THOMPSON, J.C.	September 13, 1864	South Carolina	I	26th	270

Name	Date of Death	State	Company	Regiment/Notes	Woodlawn
THOMPSON, J.P.	September 19, 1864	Virginia	G	5th	521
THOMPSON, Joel	March 29, 1865	Georgia	D	24th	2514
THOMPSON, John D.	March 12, 1865	Georgia	I	45th	2425
THOMPSON, Thomas J.	February 14, 1865	Alabama	E	1st Battalion of Artillery	2030
THOMPSON, Thomas P.	December 16, 1864	Alabama	D	13th	1062
*THOMPSON, W.A.	November 20, 1864	Georgia	G	7th Cavalry	944
THOMPSON, William	September 29, 1864	Virginia	B	48th	423
THOMPSON, William F.	February 17, 1865	South Carolina	B	24th	2230
THURSTON, Benjamin F.	September 17, 1864	Virginia	G	26th	157
THURSTON, J.W.	February 17, 1865	South Carolina	D	4th Cavalry	2229
TICE, George W.	October 30, 1864	Alabama	F	1st Battalion of Artillery	743
TIDD, William B.	December 21, 1864	Virginia	A	27th	1080
TIMMONS, John M.	December 16, 1864	South Carolina	I	18th	1270
TINDALL, Calvin	March 4, 1865	North Carolina	C	36th	1992
TINDALL, Roderick	December 5, 1864	Texas	A	1st Cavalry	1015
TINER, James	March 13, 1865	North Carolina	E	52nd	1827
TINSBLOOM, John L.	December 14, 1864	Virginia	F	55th	1123
TIPPIN, T.S.	May 9, 1865	South Carolina	F	17th	2779
TIPTON, Charles G.	December 9, 1864	Florida	F	11th - Sergeant	1038
TOBIAS, John S.	February 23, 1865	South Carolina	I	25th	2244
TODD, Bryan	April 7, 1865	North Carolina	A	1st	2652

Name	Date of Death	State	Company	Regiment/Notes	Woodlawn
TOLIVER, Solomon	September 11, 1864	North Carolina	I	61st	259
TOMBERLIN, Henry	October 1, 1864	Georgia	E	49th	410
TOMLINSON, Joseph	November 3, 1864	Virginia	D	26th Battalion	757
TOMLINSON, Manson	September 19, 1864	Virginia	H	4th	502
TOWLER, J.R.	January 25, 1865	Alabama	K	15th	1639
TOWNSEND, J.S.	January 21, 1865	North Carolina	A	23rd	1532
TRACEY, James A.	April 26, 1865	Virginia	G	31st	1427
TRAIL, Peter	December 8, 1864	Virginia	E	23rd Battalion	1162
TREADAWAY, Elijah	November 12, 1864	Mississippi	G	26th	794
TREADWELL, H.B.	September 3, 1864	Georgia	F	16th	67
TRIFFORD, Henry	September 19, 1864	Virginia	B	6th – Corporal	319
TROUTMAN, W.H.	April 21, 1865	North Carolina	H	8th	1391
TROXEL, W.J.	January 16, 1865	Tennessee	B	1st	1451
TROXLER, William	September 25, 1865	North Carolina	A	53rd	361
TUCKER, C.	December 11, 1864	Florida	A	Norwood's Miltia	1057
*TUCKER, G.W.	December 9, 1864	Alabama	F	1st Battalion of Artillery	1175
TUNE, Thomas	April 1, 1865	North Carolina	F	36th	2574
TUNE, W.S.	September 3, 1864	Virginia	C	Young's Battalion	69
TUNMIRE, D.L.	September 14, 1864	North Carolina	B	37th	279
TURNER, David W.	January 12/, 1865	North Carolina	C	51st	1480
TURNER, Elisha	February 27, 1865	Georgia	E	7th Cavalry	2153
TURNER, John	March 8, 1865	North Carolina	H	36th	2385

Name	Date of Death	State	Company	Regiment/Notes	Woodlawn
TURNER, Martin L.	September 17, 1864	Virginia	D	44th	308
TURNER, William H.	January 6, 1865	North Carolina	D	31st	1241
TURNOR, James G.	January 21, 1865	Georgia	C	12th	1591
TURR, J.B.	March 10, 1865	North Carolina	K	10th	2016
TUTEROW, T.P.	January 23, 1865	South Carolina	M	7th Cavalry	1603
TUTTLE, David	March 7, 1865	Alabama	F	1st Battalion of Artillery	2391
TWIDDY, Uriah	December 23, 1864	North Carolina	A	32nd	1097
TYNER, William	July 18, 1864	North Carolina	F	51st	2853
TYSON, George W.	March 6, 1865	North Carolina	F	22nd	1962
UMBARGER, James H.	September 14, 1864	Virginia	G	4th	285
UNDERWOOD, Benjamin F.	February 17, 1865	Georgia	B	45th	2227
UNDERWOOD, F.	January 28, 1865	Tennessee	A	1st	1655
UNDERWOOD, Jesse	January 7, 1865	Virginia	B	42nd	1231
UNDERWOOD, Jesse	February 4, 1865	Virginia	H	60th	1742
UPTON, Robert	April 3, 1865	North Carolina	F	18th	2570
*VAIN, C.R.	October 29, 1864	North Carolina	K	1st – 1st Sergeant	729
VAN HORN, Joseph	January 16, 1865	North Carolina	E	16th	1438
VANCANNON, William	July 7, 1865	North Carolina	E	3rd - Corporal	2842
VAUGHAN, Henry	July 15, 1864	Virginia	E	47th	Shohola
VAUGHAN, Jasper N.	February 5, 1865	Tennessee	C	23rd	1901
VAUGHAN, Robert D.L.	February 25, 1865	Georgia	H	24th	2290
VEST, S. S.	February 23, 1865	North Carolina	G	33rd	2245

The Confederate Prisoners' Monument.

Name	Date of Death	State	Company	Regiment/Notes	Woodlawn
VICKRY, M.A.	November 16, 1864	North Carolina	F	32nd	798
VILLEPIGUE, C.L.	February 4, 1865	South Carolina	A	7th Cavalry	1741
VINES, Chesley D.	March 20, 1865	Alabama	E	61st	1575
VINES, William Henry	December 2, 1864	Alabama	F	1st Battalion of Artillery	1006
VINSON, David J.	March 16, 1865	North Carolina	F	10th	1701
VINSON, J.B.	November 29, 1864	Alabama	F	1st Battalion of Artillery	986
VINSON, P.J.	January 6, 1865	Alabama	F	1st Battalion of Artillery	1253
VINSON, Uriah	March 19, 1865	North Carolina	I	10th	1581
VOCELLE, Augustus	March 21, 1865	South Carolina	F	25th	1527
WADE, Allen A.	March 2, 1865	North Carolina	D	3rd Cavalry	2010
WAGNER, Andrew J.	December 29, 1864	Tennessee	D	44th	1314
WAGNER, J.W.	January 5, 1865	North Carolina	D	33rd	1236
WAINWRIGHT, John	November 18, 1864	North Carolina	A	3rd	968
WALDROP, R.	October 5, 1864	Virginia	G	25th	643
WALKER, David J.	March 21, 1865	North Carolina	G	36th	1533
WALKER, Elisha	October 15, 1864	Georgia	F	14th	563
WALKER, Green	September 12, 1864	Georgia	F	49th	265
WALKER, Henry G.	January 1, 1865	North Carolina	D	42nd - Sergeant	1324
WALKER, Hezekiah	December 10, 1864	Virginia	F	29th	1156
WALKER, J.D.	March 13, 1865	Georgia	K	16th	1829
WALKER, J.R.	December 17, 1864	Georgia	B	64th	1273
WALKER, J.S.	March 4, 1865	North Carolina	F	23rd	2003

Name	Date of Death	State	Company	Regiment/Notes	Woodlawn
WALKER, Joel H.	September 28, 1864	North Carolina	H	31st	442
WALKER, John	January 30, 1865	Georgia	B	7th Cavalry	1789
WALKER, John F.	October 7, 1864	Virginia	H	25th	582
WALKER, L. D.	January 14, 1865	Alabama	A	1st Battalion of Artillery-Corporal	1460
WALKER, W. C.	March 20, 1865	Alabama	F	1st Battalion of Artillery	1567
WALKER, William F.	April 19, 1865	South Carolina	K	Holcombe Legion	1373
WALL, John R.	September 20, 1864	North Carolina	C	24th	343
WALL, Milton D. C.	November 23, 1864	Georgia	E	24th	925
WALLACE, Albert G.	October 8, 1864	Virginia	H	44th	656
WALLACE, Daniel	March 5, 1865	Alabama	A	1st Battalion of Artillery	1973
WALLACE, H. W.	February 18, 1865	North Carolina	G	26th	2359
WALLACE, Robert	September 30, 1864	North Carolina	C	35th	397
WALSH, Henry	April 18, 1865	North Carolina	K	63rd	1348
WALSH, Murphy S.	January 26, 1865	North Carolina	G	1st	1627
WALSH, William	September 24, 1864	North Carolina	K	53rd - Corporal	464
WALSTON, Jarratt	March 15, 1865	North Carolina	K	1st	1681
WALTERS, A.M.	February 20, 1865	Louisiana	D	7th	2315
WALTON, T.M.	November 5, 1864	North Carolina	B	22nd	765
WAMBLE, Albert	March 15, 1865	North Carolina	I	41st	1663
WARBURTON, M.	April 10, 1865	Virginia	A	Richmond Howitzers	2687
WARD, Alfred C.	January 22, 1865	North Carolina	B	45th	1597
WARD, Andrew I.	October 2, 1864	South Carolina	G	27th	416

Name	Date of Death	State	Company	Regiment/Notes	Woodlawn
WARD, Hardy	December 25, 1864	Alabama	E	1st Battalion of Artillery	1291
WARD, James	January 18, 1865	Alabama	E	1st Battalion of Artillery	1492
WARD, James H.	August 27, 1864	North Carolina	I	57th	104
WARD, James M.	March 17, 1865	North Carolina	G	36th	1556
WARD, Lawrence M.	December 10, 1864	North Carolina	F	24th	1044
WARD, Lorenzo	May 10, 1865	North Carolina	A	37th	2784
WARD, Melvin C.	February 22, 1865	Virginia	A	50th	2240
WARD, Oran W.	December 24, 1864	North Carolina	A	24th	1093
WARD, William J.	October 6, 1864	North Carolina	G	28th	597
WARRACH, William R.	May 22, 1865	Virginia	C	8th Cavalry	2934
*WARREN, B. F.	January 29, 1865	Virginia	C	5th Cavalry	1808
WARREN, Bluford	February 2, 1865	Virginia	F	50th	1753
WARREN, L. L.	February 20, 1865	North Carolina	F	32nd	2339
WARRING, Robert	September 22, 1864	Virginia		Citizen of Virginia	480
WARWICK, W. H.	February 26, 1865	North Carolina	F	10th	2147
WATERS, A. V.	September 17, 1864	Georgia	A	7th	172
WATERS, T. W.	April 17, 1865	Georgia	F	3rd-Sharpshooters-Sergeant	1364
*WATKINS, J.M.	August 26, 1864	North Carolina	C	14th	108
WATKINS, William B.	September 12, 1864	Virginia	H	55th	185
WATSON, N. S.	March 18, 1865	North Carolina	E	45th	1722
WATSON, Samuel D.	July 15, 1864	North Carolina	F	51st – Sergeant	Shohola

Name	Date of Death	State	Company	Regiment/Notes	Woodlawn
WATSON, William L.	February 27, 1865	Alabama	C	61st	2141
*WAY, George M.T.	July 25, 1864	Georgia	G	38th	2850
WEATHERBITE, G.	September 25, 1864	Georgia	I	38th	368
WEAVER, E.	September 20, 1864	North Carolina		Citizen of North Carolina	506
WEAVER, John R.	September 5, 1864	Virginia	K	21st	241
WEAVER, W. H.	September 15, 1864	Alabama	F	5th	293
WEBB, Alvin C.	January 8, 1865	North Carolina	E	45th	1226
WEBB, Elias S.	February 9, 1865	North Carolina	E	52nd	1950
WEBB, Nathaniel	October 2, 1864	North Carolina	D	2nd	628
WEBB, W. A.	September 14, 1864	Georgia	D	7th Cavalry	283
WEBB, William H.	December 9, 1864	Virginia	F	26th	1165
WECKLING, F.	October 1, 1864	South Carolina	L	1st	415
WEEKS, William H.	September 15, 1864	Georgia	K	49th	289
WELCH, James T.	November 16, 1864	Alabama	F	1st Battalion of Artillery	958
WELCH, John	March 2, 1865	North Carolina	G	40th	1524
WELCH, John F.	December 21, 1864	Alabama	C	1st Battalion of Artillery	1796
WELCH, W.H.	May 1, 1865	Alabama	F	1st Artillery	2737
WELLONS, William F.	February 8, 1865	Georgia	D	64th	1933
WELLS, Jacob	February 15, 1865	North Carolina	D	36th	2171
WELLS, Lee S.	September 28, 1864	Virginia	G	59th	441
WEST, Alexander	October 17, 1864	North Carolina	I	23rd	550
WEST, James	February 3, 1865	South Carolina	I	Holcombe Legion	1954
WEST, James M.	March 28, 1865	Alabama	H	48th	2492

Name	Date of Death	State	Company	Regiment/Notes	Woodlawn
WEST, John W.	October 22, 1864	Virginia	G	34th	872
WEST, W. F.	March 2, 1865	Virginia	B	15th - Corporal	2024
WEST, Washington	December 9, 1864	Virginia	G	4th Artillery	1173
WEST, William J.	April 9, 1865	North Carolina	I	36th	2614
WESTBROOK, William	March 10, 1865	Louisiana	F	3rd Cavalry	1867
WESTMORELAND, J.G.	December 10, 1864	South Carolina	I	Holcombe Legion	1040
WESTON, Richard	September 23, 1864	North Carolina	E	3rd	477
WESTREY, R.	June 7, 1865	North Carolina	H	32nd	2890
WETHERMAN, Barth H.	December 12, 1864	North Carolina	I	28th	1139
WHALEN, Rody	October 4, 1864	South Carolina	H	27th	598
WHALLEN, E.	October 22, 1864	North Carolina	I	26th	867
WHEELER, C.	May 3, 1865	North Carolina	D	36th	2748
WHEELER, James E.	October 5, 1864	Virginia	G	52nd	603
WHEELER, James F.	March 25, 1865	Georgia	D	24th	2457
WHISMAN, James W.	January 12, 1865	Virginia	A	50th	1479
WHITE, A.J.	January 13, 1865	Virginia	B	21st Cavalry	1478
WHITE, C.J.	September 1, 1864	South Carolina	K	18th	89
*WHITE, E.M.	April 23, 1865	North Carolina	K	40th	1401
WHITE, Garnett	July 27, 1865	Georgia	H	38th	2859
WHITE, George W.	January 9, 1865	Georgia	D	12th	1211
WHITE, John T.	January 12, 1865	Virginia	E	26th	1486

Name	Date of Death	State	Company	Regiment/Notes	Woodlawn
WHITE, Peter	December 23, 1864	Georgia	C	7th	1099
WHITE, Robert	March 17, 1865	Virginia	B	1st Cavalry	1698
WHITE, W. C.	November 19, 1864	Georgia	A	Legion	945
WHITE, W. S.	September 20, 1864	Virginia	F	50th	508
WHITE, William B.	March 19, 1865	Alabama	I	59th	1721
WHITE, William J.	October 5, 1864	South Carolina	B	18th	608
WHITE, William S.	October 2, 1864	Virginia	A	20th	422
WHITEHART, Willis	September 13, 1864	North Carolina	G	13th	266
WHITEHEAD, Eli M.	April 10, 1865	North Carolina	F	36th	2665
WHITEHURST, William	February 2, 1865	North Carolina	B	32nd	2577
WHITEMORE, David H.	October 18, 1864	Virginia		25th	545
WHITTAKER, B. F.	September 11, 1864	South Carolina	I	17th	251
WHITTAKER, E.B.	February 19, 1865	Alabama	A	1st Battalion of Artillery-Corporal	2344
WHITTIKER, Byrd	April 23, 1865	Virginia	H	60th	1404
WHITTINGTON, S. E.	October 23, 1864	North Carolina	I	32nd	866
WHITTON, Horace	October 2, 1864	Georgia	D	4th	618
WICKER, S.E.	September 14, 1864	North Carolina	D	57th	286
WICKLINE, D.	February 22, 1865	Virginia	A	26th	2300
WIGGINS, John C.	November 15, 1864	North Carolina	G	3rd	952
WIGGINS, Leonard E.	February 7, 1865	North Carolina	K	20th	1917
WIGGINTON, Robert A.	December 10, 1864	South Carolina	A	1st Rifles	1095
WIGGS, Haywood	April 8, 1865	North Carolina	K	43rd	2651

Name	Date of Death	State	Company	Regiment/Notes	Woodlawn
WILCOX, Reddin	November 28, 1864	North Carolina	E	51st	989
WILDER, Benjamin	March 16, 1865	South Carolina	K	25th	1693
WILDER, L.	February 2, 1865	South Carolina	K	25th	2575
WILES, William	May 11, 1865	South Carolina	F	25th	2795
*WILEY, Thomas S.	November 30, 1864	South Carolina	D	17th - Corporal	994
WILKINS, S. S.	August 1, 1864	North Carolina	C	51st	145
WILKINSON, Samuel	January 30, 1865	North Carolina	B	18th	1813
WILKINSON, W. H.	February 16, 1865	North Carolina	E	32nd	2211
WILLABY, Solomon C.	October 7, 1864	Georgia	H	44th	589
WILLETS, J.L.	April 14, 1865	North Carolina	G	36th	2707
WILLETS, John J.	May 7, 1865	North Carolina	G	36th	2770
WILLETS, W.J.	March 4, 1865	North Carolina	G	26th	1977
WILLIAMS, A. W.	April 20, 1865	South Carolina	D	21st	1379
WILLIAMS, Alex	September 6, 1864	Virginia	D	26th	244
WILLIAMS, Anthony M.	January 6, 1865	Virginia	I	11th Cavalry	1230
WILLIAMS, B.	January 11, 1865	Georgia	K	Macon Artillery	1213
WILLIAMS, Gilbert	December 3, 1864	North Carolina	A	18th	888
WILLIAMS, Harrison	November 7, 1864	Georgia	A	35th	768
WILLIAMS, J.A.	April 22, 1865	Alabama	F	1st Battalion of Artillery	1396
WILLIAMS, J.A.	September 17, 1864	North Carolina	B	31st	150
WILLIAMS, J.H.	April 3, 1865	North Carolina	D	1st	2550
WILLIAMS, J.H.	February 4, 1865	North Carolina	C	45th	2560

Name	Date of Death	State	Company	Regiment/Notes	Woodlawn
WILLIAMS, J.W.	March 24, 1865	North Carolina	K	40th	2458
WILLIAMS, James H.	October 29, 1864	North Carolina	H	45th	728
WILLIAMS, James H.	July 15, 1864	Georgia	K	53rd	Shohola
WILLIAMS, James M.	January 18, 1865	Virginia	F	29th	1210
WILLIAMS, James W.	January 19, 1865	North Carolina	G	45th	1206
WILLIAMS, Joel	March 4, 1865	North Carolina	E	36th	1972
WILLIAMS, John	October 28, 1864	North Carolina	E	2nd	725
WILLIAMS, John R.	March 13, 1865	Virginia	Page's Company		1833
WILLIAMS, Rufus F.	October 19, 1864	Virginia	D	26th - Sergeant	536
WILLIAMS, Samuel	August 20, 1864	North Carolina	B	52nd	113
WILLIAMS, Thomas H.	September 26, 1864	Georgia	A	60th - Sergeant	451
WILLIAMS, W.	October 1, 1864	South Carolina	M	7th	409
WILLIAMS, Weldon	February 4, 1865	Louisiana	D	6th	1886
WILLIAMS, William B.	May 10, 1865	Virginia	I	50th	2787
WILLIAMS, William W.	October 24, 1864	Alabama	E	1st Battalion Artillery	709
WILLIAMSON, E. S.	March 14, 1865	North Carolina	E	36th	1674
WILLIAMSON, J. R.	February 15, 1865	North Carolina	E	36th	2183
WILLIAMSON, James	April 11, 1865	North Carolina	E	34th	2692
WILLIAMSON, James	March 15, 1865	South Carolina	B	21st	1690
WILLIAMSON, Joshua W.	June 21, 1865	North Carolina	E	36th	2813
WILLIAMSON, R.M.	December 31, 1864	Georgia	B	7th Cavalry	1326

Name	Date of Death	State	Company	Regiment/Notes	Woodlawn
WILLIAMSON, Walker	October 10, 1864	Virginia	G	4th	670
WILLIS, Henry P.	August 20, 1864	Virginia	F	30th	112
WILSON, D.C.	March 22, 1865	North Carolina	E	41st, 3rd Cavalry-State Troop	2440
WILSON, Daniel	December 9, 1864	South Carolina	B	7th	1036
WILSON, Frank M.	February 25, 1865	Alabama	G	10th	2278
WILSON, George	April 7, 1865	Virginia	B	11th Cavalry	2650
WILSON, Gray D.	September 23, 1864	Virginia	B	42nd	476
WILSON, I.W.	February 3, 1865	North Carolina	D	36th	2565
WILSON, J.B.	January 23, 1865	South Carolina	K	Holcombe Legion	1609
WILSON, Obadiah	March 24, 1865	Virginia	E	19th - Corporal	2447
WILSON, R.L.	February 4, 1865	North Carolina	H	35th	1891
WILSON, Richard	February 11, 1865	Maryland	A	1st Cavalry	2082
WILSON, W.C.	March 24, 1865	South Carolina	K	21st	2450
WILSON, Zeo B.	September 15, 1864	North Carolina	G	28th	300
WINGATE, T.J.	September 12, 1864	Florida	K	2nd Cavalry	379
WINKLER, A.W.	February 15, 1865	Louisiana	K	6th	2165
WINKLER, Abraham	March 5, 1865	Tennessee	D	7th	2410
WINN, H.	September 29, 1864	South Carolina	D	1st	424
WINSTON, James H.	December 17, 1864	Louisiana	E	20th	1278
WISE, William	November 4, 1864	Tennessee	B	14th	839
WISEMAN, J.C.	June 23, 1865	Alabama	H	6th	2819

Name	Date of Death	State	Company	Regiment/Notes	Woodlawn
WISHER, J.	May 18, 1865	South Carolina	C	17th	2948
WITHERS, James D.	September 26, 1864	North Carolina	I	1st	371
WITHROW, James W.	February 25, 1865	Virginia	H	25th	2274
WOFORD, Thomas	March 17, 1865	South Carolina	F	13th	1712
WOLF, D.W.	March 1, 1865	South Carolina	G	25th	2100
WOMACK, H.N.	April 21, 1865	North Carolina	K	5th	1387
WOMACK, L.H.	April 9, 1865	Tennessee	K	44th	2625
WOOD, E.M.	January 20, 1865	Alabama	F	1st Battalion of Artillery	1641
WOOD, Ferney	November 4, 1864	North Carolina	B	56th	840
WOOD, M.A.	December 26, 1864	South Carolina	C	22nd	1289
WOOD, Miles	February 21/65	Alabama	E	1st Battalion of Artillery	2296
WOOD, W.H.	May 23, 1865	Virginia	B	15th	2927
WOOD, William F.	October 24, 1864	Alabama	F	1st Battalion of Artillery	712
WOODALL, Samuel	November 21, 1864	Virginia	H	42nd	975
WOODARD, Abram	March 25, 1865	Virginia	B	48th	2463
WOODARD, John A.	February 7, 1865	North Carolina	H	36th	1927
WOODHAM, I.A.	June 4, 1865	Alabama	G	15th	2897
*WOODLAND, J.H.	February 23, 1865	Virginia	A	26th	2263
WOODS, David B.	December 28, 1864	Virginia	F	25th	1302
WOODS, John R.	February 17, 1865	Georgia	C	38th	2357
WOODSIDE, Isaiah W.	December 17, 1864	Virginia	A	25th	1284

Name	Date of Death	State	Company	Regiment/Notes	Woodlawn
WOODWARD, T.J.	September 19, 1864	South Carolina	G	27th	501
WOODWORTH, A.	November 26, 1864	Virginia	G	15th Cavalry	976
WOODY, R.L.	April 28, 1865	Virginia	B	15th - Corporal	2727
WOOLFE, Charles B.	September 11, 1864	Virginia	E	50th	256
WOOSLEY, W.H.	November 6, 1864	North Carolina	E	33rd	771
WORD, John	March 11, 1865	North Carolina	F	10th Artillery	1843
WORKMAN, James L.	January 22, 1865	North Carolina	K	12th	1589
WORKMAN, Sidney	February 1, 1865	North Carolina	G	28th	1755
WORMINGTON, James	March 17, 1865	North Carolina	H	8th	1706
WORRELL, A.	March 16, 1865	Virginia	I	50th	1682
WORRELL, Irvin	February 10, 1865	North Carolina	F	10th	1947
WORSHAM, J.K.	February 24, 1865	South Carolina	I	25th	2241
*WORSHAM, R.M.	April 8, 1865	Georgia	H	60th	2624
WORTHAM, W.A.	February 13, 1865	Virginia	G	4th	2038
WREN, William	October 2, 1864	North Carolina	E	35th	626
WRENN, James I.	September 17, 1864	Virginia		Citizen of Virginia	167
WRENN, T.N.	November 18, 1864	South Carolina	A	61st	963
WRIGHT, David F.	October 18, 1864	Alabama	B	61st - Sergeant	542
WRIGHT, Henry	March 30, 1865	Virginia	G	47th	2530
WRIGHT, J.M.	October 20, 1864	South Carolina	H	18th	525
WRIGHT, J.P.	April 9, 1865	South Carolina	H	22nd	2611

Name	Date of Death	State	Company	Regiment/Notes	Woodlawn-
WRIGHT, James L.	April 18, 1865	North Carolina	K	10th Artillery	1365
WRIGHT, W.T.	December 17, 1864	Tennessee	B	1st Artillery	1282
WRIGHT, William	September 20, 1864	North Carolina	F	6th	326
WYATT, John W.	September 15, 1864	Virginia	F	42nd	277
WYATT, William M.	October 24, 1864	Virginia	G	26th	857
WYNN, Thomas D.	April 7, 1865	North Carolina	H	1st	2640
YARBENY, E.S.	July 17, 1865	Alabama	E	13th	2871
YARBOROUGH, H.	March 10, 1865	Louisiana	B	10th Battalion	1866
YARBOROUGH, T.Y.	April 28, 1865	South Carolina	B	21st Artillery	2728
YATES, Daniel	April 3, 1865	North Carolina	H	1st	2559
YORK, Eli	September 16, 1864	North Carolina	A	53rd	306
YOUNG, Harrison	September 17, 1864	Virginia	D	24th	163
YOUNG, James	April 5, 1865	Alabama	E	1st Artillery	2543
YOUNG, James A. B.	August 15, 1864	South Carolina	G	1st	28
YOUNG, Martin A.	March 1, 1865	North Carolina	E	6th Cavalry	1994
YOUNG, William F.	April 24, 1865	North Carolina	H	3rd - Corporal	1406
YOUNGBLOOD, Nathaniel M.	February 26, 1865	Alabama	C	1st Battalion of Artillery	2132
YOUNGBLOOD, S. A.	March 8, 1865	South Carolina	D	14th	2368
YOUNGER, William	January 25, 1865	North Carolina	I	45th	1617
ZEBE, J.H.	October 24, 1864	South Carolina	E	11th	

Name	Date of Death	State	Company	Regiment/Notes	Woodlawn
UNKNOWN	March 18, 1865				1558
UNKNOWN					1814
UNKNOWN					2026
UNKNOWN					2049
UNKNOWN					2481
UNKNOWN					2482

MEMORIAL DAY ODE

The past is dead, long live the past;
And may its memory ever last
In hearts through which the Southern blood
Leaps on its way an untamed flood.
For we who bear the Southern name
Look on the past and find no shame
Attached to the cause which, though lost,
Was worth the life-blood which it cost.
And though the mournful willows wave
Over the low mounds which we lave
With bitter tears, we feel,
We know the future will reveal
That each martyred hero doth wear
A crown of heavenly laurel fair.
Each spot which heard the dying moans,
And which in death received the bones
Of those who freely gave their all,
In answer to the Southland's call -
No matter where they may be found,
Such spots are sacred, holy ground.
The heroes who sleep 'neath the sods
Rest in sweet peace, their souls are God's,
Until the Judgment trump be blown,
And wrong forever is o'erthrown;
Then they will rise up one and all
To answer to the Last Roll Call.

Reverend G. R. ROOD
MILLBROOK, North Carolina
May 7, 1904

Alternate information
Names

BARMAN, Jonas also known as Bowman, Jonas

BARNHILL, D.R. also known as Barnill, Duncan

BEATTY, C.B. first name Cephus, actually from North Carolina

BENFIELD, R.A. first name Riley, actually from 32nd Regiment, Co F North Carolina

BENTON, Theodore also known as Benton, Thomas

BLANTON, J.J. also known as Blanton, James Joseph

BOIE, Mitchell also known as Buie, Mitchell

BOLES, Richard also known as Bowles, Richard

BOTTS, F.A. should be BOTTS, Thomas A., known as "Buttons"

BRINKLEY, Fetherd also known as Brinkly, Jethro K.

BROOKS, D.H. also known as Brooks, David H.

BROOKS, J.H. also known as Brooks, John W.

BURK, Isaac also known as Burke, Isaac

BURKET John also known as Burkett, John

CLAYTON, William T. Goodwin's Militia should be Florida Militia

CLEMENTS, B.B. also known as Clements, Bedford Booker

COCHRAN, A.W. also known as Cochran, Allen

COCHRAN, John also known as Cockerham, John

COLEY, Wesley also known as Cooley, William

COLLINS, John also known as Callis, John

CORDER, D.A. also known as Corders, David

CREEKMORE, M. also known as Creekmore, Malachi

DEAN, John also known as Deans, John

DODDRIDGE, W. should be Daughtrige, Willey

DRY, J. A. should be Dry, Tobias Augustus

ELLISON, James also known as Allison, James

EVANS, J. A. also known as Evans, John Albert

FAULKNER, W. L. also known as Falkner, William Leonidas

FLANAGAN, Barney also known as Flannegan, Barney
FORTHEWIS, Lewis should be Fortlouis, Michel
FOSTER, Thomas also known as Forrester, Thomas
FOWLER, J. S. also known as Fowler, John
GAMBLE, F. E. also known as Gamble, Thomas E.
HAILEY, H. A also known as Haley, Harvey V.
HALEY, H. also known as Haley, Andrew Jackson
HENDRICK, Levi actual last name is Hedrick
HOWE, J.T. also known as Howe, John T.
HOWE, Nathanial L. also known as Howe, Nathan
HUDSON, J. B. sometimes listed as Hulson, J. B.
JERNEGAN, G.W. also known as Jernegan, George W.
JOB, Jesse R. also known as Jobe, Jesse R.
JOHNSON, J. L. questionable listing - there was a G Company in Louisiana but Power's Regiment was in Mississippi not Louisiana
KELLIHER, Dennis also known as Kelliher, Daniel
KINLAW, Neil also known as Kinlaw, Neill
LAFFMAN, William sometimes listed as Luffman, William
LARMAN, Joseph also known as Lowman, Joseph
LINDSAY, E.H. also known as Lindsay, E. K.
MANEY, O.H. actual name was Maxey, Obediah Henry
McGOWEN, Daniel S. also known as McKeown, Daniel S.
McWALTERS, John sometimes listed as McWaters, John
McWATTERS, John also known as McWatters, Jesse
NEAL, W.C. also known as Neal, William
PARKER, James P. actually in Company A
PERYMORE, L. B. sometimes known as Parmore, L.B.
OWENS, D. also known as Owens, Dempsey
RAWLS, James L. also known as Rawls, James M.
REDDING, Alf also known as Redding, Alfred
RICKMAN, J.J. also known as Rickman, John

SADDLER/SADLER, William was from South Carolina not North Carolina
SELLERS, W. R. also known as Sellers, W. Riley
SIMMONS, H. actual first name Noah
SIMMONS, J. F. also known as Simmons, John F.
SMITH, Fred also known as Smith, Frederick
SMITH, T. John preferred to be called "John Smith T"
SPARKMAN, W. P. also known as Sparkman, William
STINSON, L. also known as Stinson, George Leander
STURGEON, H. also known as Sturgeon, Hiram
SUMNERS, Matthew also known as Sumner, Matthew
TAYLOR, David B. also known as Taylor, David D.
TAYLOR, J.J. also known as Taylor, Joseph J.
TEAGUE, O.S. also known as Teague, Oliver Sanford
THOMPSON, W.A. also known as Thompson, William A.
TUCKER, G.W. also known as Tucker, George Washington
VAIN, C.R also known as Vann, Chester R.
WARREN, B. F also known as Warren, Burris
WATKINS, J.M. also known as Watkins, James
WHITE, E.M should be Musselwhite, Eli
WILEY, Thomas S. also known as Wiley, Sumpter
WOODLAND, J.H. also known as Woodland, James
WORSHAM, R.M. also known as Worsham, Robert A.

Alternate information
Dates

Surmising from the Woodlawn Cemetery marker numbers these death dates seem more correct, or possibly these remains were disinterred from the Prison Camp location and moved to Woodlawn National Cemetery in 1865.

CAMPBELL, John possibly died July 15, 1865 not 1864
GRAHAM, Daniel possibly died July 24, 1865 not 1864
HURT, Thomas possibly died July 22, 1865 not 1864
MEREDITH, John possibly died March 6 not May 6, 1865
PATE, Able possibly died in March 5, 1865 not May 5, 1865
PREVETT, Abner possibly died July 5, 1865 not 1864
ROBERTS, William possibly died July 25, 1865 not 1864
ROMINES, James possibly died July 18, 1865 not 1864
STOCKDALE, William possibly died July 9, 1865 not 1864
WAY, George M. T. possibly died July 25, 1865 not 1864

Bibliography

"Civil War Soldiers and Sailors System Search Form." September 2, 2007 <http://www.itd.nps.gov/cwss/Personz_Search1.cfm>.

Costello, Brian. March 20, 21, 2006. personal e-mails.

Ellis, John. "WS_FTP\csn\elmira." 2000. Confederate Navy Research Center. May 30, 2008 <http://www.csnavy.org/ny/elmira.htm>.

Courtney, Richard. "South Carolina Civil War - Soldiers in Prisons." 1998. RootsWeb. January 3, 2008 <http://www.rootsweb.ancestry.com/~scwbts/prisoners.htm>.

"Elmira Prison Camp." May 21, 2008 <http://www.factasy.com/civil_war/elmira>.

Evans, John E. "Henry Evans." December 10, 11, 2008. Personal e-mails.

Hartshorn, Derick S. "Catawba County, NC Soldiers Buried at Elmira." 2008. April 20, 2009 <http://www.catawbascv.org/Elmira.htm>.

Hathcock, Art. "Calvin Hathcock." December 3, 2008. Personal e-mail.

Howard, Randall. "1st Battalion, Alabama Artillery." October 27, 2008 <www.angelfire.com/tx3/RandysTexas/1stalabama.html>.

Ironmonger, Chuck. "Chemung County History please." April 28, 2009. personal e-mail.

Jernigan, T. Watson. Death At Elmira: George W. Jernigan, William Hoffman, and The Union Prison System. 2005. East Tennessee State University/Jernigan. East Tennessee State University. March 24, 2008 <http://etd-submit.etsu.edu/etd/theses/available/etd-0404105-082855/unrestricted/JerniganTW042505f.pdf>.

"Lincoln, Abraham - Proclamation of Amnesty and Reconstruction." February 19, 2008 <http://www.classicallibrary.org/lincoln/reconstruction.htm>.

Parker, Cynthia, M. Ed. "Ancestors and Elmira Prison Camp." December 6, 2008. Personal e-mail.

Scott, Brian. "Elmira Prison Camp OnLine Library." May 13, 2008 <http://www.angelfire.com/ny5/elmiraprison/index.html>.

Shaw, James. "Chemung County History." December 6, 2009. Personal email.

Taylor, Wayne. "J M. page." August 31, 2008 <http://www.geocities.com/gomezadams2/JM.html>.

Taylor, Wayne. "Marshall Taylor." May 2, 2008. Personal e-mail.

Taylor, Wayne. "J M." May 2, 2008 <http://www.geocities.com/gomezadams2/JM.html>.

Tew, Jerome. Email correspondence. March 15, 16, 17, 2008.

"The Great Shohola Train Wreck." www.shohola.com. December 29, 2006 <http://www.shohola.com/trainwreck/>.

"The War for Southern Independence - the Civil War in Florida - Military Units formed in Florida." March 22, 2008 <http://www.researchonline.net/flcw/flunits.htm>.

"Woodlawn National Cemetery Surnames." Interment.net. July 7, 2007 <http://www.interment.net/data/us/ny/chemung/woodnat/index.htm>.

The Elmira Prison Camp officially closed on July 5, 1865. The last prisoner buried was number 2963 - H. J. F. Griffin who died on March 16, 1865 during the time of the Chemung River flood five months previous.

New York History Review

www.NewYorkHistoryReview.com

www.ingramcontent.com/pod-product-compliance
Lightning Source LLC
Chambersburg PA
CBHW020757160426
43192CB00006B/350